JANE AUSTEN AND NAMES

Maggie Lane

Blaise Books

Published by Blaise Books, 2002
1 Brookleaze, Bristol BS9 2ET

ISBN 0-9542625-0-6

British Library Catalogue-in-Publication Data: a catalogue record for this book is available from the British Library

Typeset, printed and bound by Burleigh Press, Bristol

To my daughter Emily

who shares my passion for names

Also by Maggie Lane

The Jane Austen Quiz and Puzzle Book

Jane Austen's Family Through Five Generations

Jane Austen's England

Literary Daughters

A Charming Place: Bath in the Life and Novels of Jane Austen

Jane Austen and Food

Jane Austen's World

A City of Palaces: Bath Through the Eyes of Fanny Burney

Contents

"I wish young ladies had not such a number of fine Christian names"

Persuasion

Preface, Bibliography and Acknowledgements

This book is about the Christian names used by Jane Austen in her mature fiction. By this I mean the six novels - *Sense and Sensibility*, *Pride and Prejudice*, *Northanger Abbey*, *Mansfield Park*, *Emma* and *Persuasion*, plus the novella *Lady Susan* and the fragments *The Watsons and Sanditon.* Let other pens dwell on surnames and place names if they will[i]: for me, only the names which a society is free to choose for itself - and to choose afresh with each generation - reveal its values, conflicts and aspirations. There is fashion in first names as in houses, manners or dress. By exploring Jane Austen's choice of such names, I hope to add a little to our understanding of the culture to which she belonged and our appreciation of her skill in manipulating the name stock which it offered for her use.

At several points I have found it pertinent to quote from *The History of Christian Names* by the Victorian novelist Charlotte Mary Yonge, published in 1863. Yonge (or CMY, as I sometimes refer to her in the text) was a lifelong admirer of Austen, and her memoirs and letters contain many references to her novels. When visiting Lyme she commented, "Of course we thought of Louisa Musgrove, as I suppose everybody does". On another occasion she spent an enjoyable evening "capping Miss Austen *con amore*" with a friend.[ii] While *The History of Christian Names* does not mention Jane Austen or any of her characters by name, it not only gives much interesting information on the history of names - Yonge's research was prodigious - but more to the purpose for my book, her mid-nineteenth century take on the subject sheds light on the tastes of the preceding generation.

For general reference I have relied on *The Oxford Dictionary of English Christian Names* by E.G. Withycombe, published by OUP in 1945 and revised in 1976, full of much fascinating historical matter. I must also mention the marvellous *First Names First* by Leslie Alan Dunkling, published by Coronet in 1978. This book was the first, and to my knowledge is still the only, study of English Christian names to focus on how people perceive names in their own era rather than on what they might have meant originally. I am only sorry that it is now out of print.

When I have quoted Jane Austen's own words they have been taken from the Clarendon edition of her novels, edited by R.W. Chapman, and from *Jane Austen's Letters* edited by Deirdre Le Faye, published by OUP in 1995 - though I have not felt constrained, in such a *jeu d'ésprit* as the present work, to give page numbers. "I do not write for such dull elves" as cannot look up references for themselves, as Jane Austen herself might have said. Because Jane Austen's niece Fanny shared her interest in names, I have also consulted *Fanny Knight's Diaries* edited by Deirdre Le Faye and published by the Jane Austen Society in 2000.

This is my first venture into self-publishing. Having formerly published some dozen books with five different publishers, my motivation was not vanity, but fun. After all, as a librarian by profession and an erstwhile antiquarian bookshop assistant, not to mention ordinary bookworm, I have read, written, lent, borrowed, bought and sold books: the only thing left to do is to publish them. My love affair with books extends to their physical properties and it has been thoroughly fascinating to follow through every process in their design and construction. Though I have always been on excellent terms with my publishers, and have learnt much from them, on this occasion I have relished making every decision myself.

Nevertheless, the process would not have been so straightforward and enjoyable without the interest and support of many friends. I would particularly like to thank Dave Baldock, Diana Birchall, Susannah Fullerton, Tim Graham, Paul Lane, Louise Ross, Emily Shepherd and Peter Troy for sharing their knowledge and helping the enterprise along in various ways. I am also grateful to my printer, Andrew Moon of Burleigh Press, for making everything go smoothly.

My warmest thanks are due to Tom Carpenter of the Jane Austen Memorial Trust for supplying in digital form and granting permission to reproduce the miniature on the front cover, the original of which may be seen at the Jane Austen House museum, Chawton, Hants. Painted around 1804, it shows two of Jane Austen's nieces, Elizabeth and Marianne Austen (later Knight), born in 1800 and 1801 respectively. They were the sixth and seventh children in a family of eleven. Elizabeth, the second daughter, was named for her mother and was always known as Lizzy. She had fifteen children herself but, unlike her mother, did not die in bringing the last one into the world. Marianne was named for a maternal aunt and lived out her long life as a maiden aunt herself, "Aunt May".

The pleasure of choosing names for progeny is one that maiden aunts normally forfeit. But not Jane Austen. She beat her sister-in-law's eleven and her niece's fifteen without any risk to her health. The fertility of her brain secured for her the pleasure, the power and perhaps the puzzle, of choosing Christian names for more than two hundred characters. How she did so, and to what effect, is what this book is all about.

[i] See 'Jane Austen's Art of Naming' by Susannah Fullerton, published in *Persuasions*, the journal of the Jane Austen Society of North America, 1997.

[ii] I am indebted to Diana Birchall, who has made a study of the connections between Austen and Yonge, for this information.

Introduction

The process by which any author selects names for his or her characters must remain largely mysterious, even to the author. The fascinating thing about Christian names – and this is the right term here, for all Jane Austen's characters are Christians - is that they have to be drawn from a limited stock. There are far fewer first names than surnames in circulation, as our own experience - or a glance through any phone book - attests. Members of a culture share a stock of known first names, from life and literature, some of which (all of which?) at any given period are associated with certain characteristics. In matching name with character, the author draws on these often subconscious associations.

Some authors also take care to choose names likely to have been borne by those characters in that time, family and milieu. With each naming, a choice has to be made between realism and originality. It is a temptation which not all authors can resist to bestow unusual or even made-up first names, especially on a heroine. Indeed, our name-stock has been enriched in this way. However, Jane Austen, as we may suppose from all we know of her, prefers what is probable. Not for her the 'Cecilia or Camilla or Belinda' that she cites in *Northanger Abbey* as heroines of sister-novelists. Catherine, Anne and Elizabeth suit her fastidious taste much better.

In the matter of Christian names, as in so many aspects of her art, she works from a limited palette - and she does so deliberately. It is true that there were far fewer names in circulation in the Georgian and Regency periods than in earlier or later times. But still there were many more names available to her than she chose to use. The more fanciful names of the juvenilia disappear when she writes her mature fiction. Even some of the names familiar to her from family and friends were rejected by her for use in novels because she knew they were uncommon. Her worthy characters have plain, unpretending names, such as would not draw attention to themselves. When it comes to the published novels, her most unusual names (Basil, Archibald, Alicia) are confined to non-speaking parts.

Though Jane Austen famously never repeats a character, she certainly does repeat names. And not only across the whole work, but within an individual novel. There are four Johns in *Sense and Sensibility* alone; three Toms and a Thomas in *Mansfield Park*; while *Persuasion* has five boys or men named Charles and four Marys.

Sometimes namesakes share leading characteristics. Her Charlottes are usually clear-eyed pragmatists and her Henrys are rarely without charm. More often, characters given the same name have nothing in common at all. In one novel Fanny might be a despicable, mercenary snob, and in another the timid, tender-hearted heroine. George Wickham and George Knightley are morally worlds apart. No fewer than three of Jane Austen's most vulgar characters are named Anne; but so too is the possessor of the most refined mind she created.

The classic English names, borne by royalty for centuries, are her staple. These seem to have registered as neutral in her mind, suitable for a variety of characters. All her brothers had names from this category, and she used them over and over again. She possessed such a name herself, choosing it for two quite major characters, without apparently feeling that her own personality got in the way of the imaginative process. But though such names predominate, her repertoire includes several other categories. When she feels it appropriate for a character to bear a fashionable or pretentious name she draws on the latinate creations of the eighteenth century (e.g. Louisa, Augusta). When she has a servant or other low-born person to name, the old biblical or saints' names (Hannah, Stephen) and outmoded diminutives (Betty instead of Elizabeth) serve her purpose. Finally some of her favourite characters bear names of a medieval stamp (Edmund, Frederick) for which she had a lifelong affection, anticipating the taste of the generation that followed hers.

In any era, the usable stock of names always consists of more female than male names, parents and authors tending to be more adventurous when naming girls. In the six published novels and three mature fragments which form the body of her work, Jane Austen uses 26 boys' names and 55 girls' names. These she repeats and distributes among the one hundred and fourteen male and one hundred and twenty-seven female characters on whom she bestows a Christian name.

There are many other characters whose first names she did not trouble to decide, or to reveal. We do not need to know the Christian names of Mr and Mrs Allen, Mr and Mrs Bennet, Colonel and Mrs Wallis or a myriad others - they are perfect as they are. But occasionally a name one would expect to learn is withheld. It seems odd that in *Persuasion* Anne's old school friend, Miss Hamilton, now Mrs Smith, is given no first name even in Anne's thoughts. She must know it; I should like to know it too, but there is no guessing it. Similarly with Mrs Dixon, *née* Campbell, in *Emma*. Jane Fairfax's reserve extends to never breathing the name of the girl who has been her companion since childhood. What a pity that Miss Bates never lets the name escape her - or 'pop out', as she would herself say.

Sometimes an educated guess *is* possible. Of the three Miss Wards, one is Maria and one Frances, but what is Mrs Norris's first name? It could well be Elizabeth, as that is what her god-daughter is called. On the same principle, we might suspect Lady Russell's name to be Anne.

Occasionally a name is bestowed which would be easy to miss, as it is mentioned only once in speech, rather than being stated by the narrator. This is how we learn that Mr Elton's name is Philip, a name that appears just once in the text of *Emma*. In the same novel Miss Bates' first name is revealed to us in a single speech by her mother, surely adding poignancy to the character. When old Mrs Bates has died, Miss Bates will never again hear herself called Hetty. She will be Miss Bates to all the world, until Mr Elton or his successor conducts her funeral service. As readers we are privileged to be given this glimpse into her girlhood, before life closed down most of its possibilities to Miss Bates. In such ways does the use of Christian names add richness to a text.

> *"There is nobleness in the name of Edmund. It is a name of heroism and renown - of kings, princes and knights; and seems to breathe the spirit of chivalry and warm affections."*
>
> **Mansfield Park**

Names and the novelist's art

In her earliest scraps of fiction, written and read aloud for family amusement, Jane Austen's intention was to poke fun at the literary fashions of the day. Her plots are absurd and her choice of names outlandish. They include Gustavus, Polydore and Philander for men, and a whole host of more or less unlikely names for women: Agatha, Amelia, Arabella, Camilla, Cecilia, Claudia, Dorothea, Elfrida, Eloisa, Janetta, Jezalinda, Laurina, Melissa and Rosa. As the youthful Jane Austen had observed, and was here parodying, novelists and playwrights of the period found it almost obligatory to choose polysyllabic names for their heroines: Henry Tilney, in seeking to prove to Catherine that he has read "hundreds and hundreds" of novels, humorously defies her to compete with him in "knowledge of Julias and Louisas". But these are tame compared with Ethelinda, Emmeline and Clarentine, all eponymous heroines of novels published in the 1790s and known to have been read by Jane Austen. She certainly understood from an early age the two prime requirements of popular literature. "Remember, whatever you do, that your hero and heroine must possess a great deal of feeling and very pretty names," runs the letter in *The Loiterer*, the periodical edited by James and Henry Austen at Oxford; signed "Sophia Sentiment", it is suspected to be by the young Jane Austen herself.

As she left aside burlesque and began to create imaginary worlds more rooted in the observable one around her, the nomenclature changed. It is true that there is still a trace of romance in the polysyllabic 'Elinor and Marianne', as we know the first version of *Sense and Sensibility* was eponymously called, and in the hero's name in 'First Impressions', which became *Pride and Prejudice*. But the rest of the *dramatis personae* in both novels bear the names of common life. By the third of the novels belonging to her first great period of creativity, *Northanger Abbey*, names are chosen almost schematically to fit family backgrounds. Of the three families, that of the heroine (herself originally called Susan) have very down-to-earth names, the Tilneys have desirably medieval names to go with their style of abode, and the Thorpes are pretentious on the female side and banal on the male.

In none of her texts is Jane Austen's choice of names either arbitrary or without significance. But some texts go further, playing games with nomenclature or extracting more than usual meaning from the very subject of names. This is most marked in the novels belonging to her Chawton period, when she was writing at the height of her powers.

In *Mansfield Park*, the lovers are more than usually aware of one another's names. The two rivals for Edmund's love, Mary Crawford and Fanny Price, discuss his name. Though all that Mary will allow is that "the name is good in itself", this is quite a concession from a woman predetermined to be rational, cool and sophisticated about matters of the heart. It shows how far she is falling under Edmund's spell. As for Fanny, she goes into positive raptures. "There is nobleness in the name of Edmund," she asserts. "It is a name of heroism and renown - of kings, princes and knights; and seems to breathe the spirit of chivalry and warm affections." She has evidently dwelt much on the name, though, strangely perhaps, we never hear her use it to address Edmund himself - he is always "cousin".

Equally, she is enthralled when he writes her own name in a short note, poring over the four words "My very dear Fanny". Conversely, she cannot bear to hear the name Fanny uttered with familiarity and fondness by the Crawfords, repulsing them both. But Henry Crawford is in that state of early love when everything about the beloved enchants him, and he has made almost a fetish of her name. "It is 'Fanny' that I think of all day, and dream of all night. - You have given the name such reality of sweetness, that nothing else can now be descriptive of you." No other male lover in the novels says anything comparable to this. Names seem to be part of the intensity of *Mansfield Park*.

Emma is a more light-hearted - though no less profound or artistically accomplished - novel, full of games and wordplay that operate on more than one level. Many of them are to do with names. The scrap of verse "Kitty a fair but frozen maid" reminds fond Mr Woodhouse of his absent daughter Isabella, "who was near being christened Catherine after her grandmama". His harmless vanity and self-centredness are illustrated by his pleasure in Isabella's eldest son's being called after him rather than his own father. Mr Weston makes a rather feeble pun on Emma's name when he invites his audience to guess which two letters of the alphabet denote perfection, and gives the answer 'MA'. Emma herself puns when she speaks of the building in which "N takes M for better or worse": these are the letters which stand in for groom and bride in the Book of Common Prayer, but they can also serve for Knightley and Emma. Mrs Elton boasts that she has had an acrostic written on her name - that is, a poem whose lines begin with the letters in AUGUSTA. Frank Churchill exploits the alphabet game for his own ends, forming the word 'Dixon', to the amusement of Emma and displeasure of Jane. "I did not know that proper names were allowed," she says in an angry spirit.

Emma famously cannot think of her future husband as George, so there are certainly no Fanny-style raptures from her. Though Mr Knightley has nothing like Henry Crawford's obsession with the name of his beloved, he does seem to enjoy pronouncing her name, which he speaks no fewer than sixty-eight times in the novel. In the first part of the book he often addresses her as "my dear Emma," as befits his customary mode of instruction or reasoning with her; but after their engagement this changes subtly but all-importantly to the more tender and equal "my Emma" or "Emma, my love".

The way names are handled contributes to the tone of each of these later novels. So there is a difference again with *Persuasion*. Here the sterility of the Kellynch family is indicated by their confining themselves to the same few names over many centuries: "all the Marys and Elizabeths they had married". They are almost incestuous in their exclusivity. "There was not a baronet from A to Z" whom the present Elizabeth desires to marry as much as the man who bears her own father's two names (plus one of his own). Even Anne is momentarily tempted to marry the same man by the thought of reviving in herself her mother's name, "Lady Elliot". This Mr Elliot, whose name is his greatest charm for both sisters, in their different ways, has come to appreciate the value of it, and exploit it. In rebellious youth he had written, "I wish I had any name but Elliot. I am sick of it. The name of Walter I can drop, thank God!" But he has not independence enough to adhere to this line; love of money and status bring him back into the fold. His name is his destiny.

In contrast, Anne earns her escape. She does this by her wider imaginative sympathy, shown in her acknowledging the good points of a different family, where the girls have "new" names; in loving a man whose name is better than his connections; and in her loyalty to an old friend fallen on hard times who has "no sirname *[sic]* of dignity". Her father's opposition to this friendship makes much of the name. "Mrs Smith, of all people and all names in the world, to be the chosen friend of Miss Anne Elliot.... Mrs Smith, such a name!" But even the noble surname of Wentworth is insufficient to recommend itself to Sir Walter, its owner having, as he discovers, "nothing to do with the Strafford family". "One wonders how the names of many of our nobility become so common," he says. All the mention of names in the novel, except Admiral Croft's comic inability to remember the fancy names of the Musgrove daughters, reinforces the impression of snobbery and constriction from which Anne must, through her own good qualities, break free.

With *Sanditon*, the fragment of a novel begun and abandoned in the last few months of Jane Austen's life, a new direction seems indicated, though at the same time there is a return to some of the burlesque qualities of the juvenilia. Appropriately, there is a little clutch of names completely new in the fiction: Esther, Clara, Diana and Sidney are all new, and Arthur almost new (just one non-speaking character in *Emma*). Set against these slightly overdrawn characters (which is where the resemblance to the juvenilia comes in) is the sane, well-judging heroine who observes them all: and she has the familiar name of Charlotte, which always signifies common sense to Jane Austen.

This leads us to the main focus of this book, consideration of the individual names in the fiction. It will be helpful to begin by looking at the history of English Christian names from before the Conquest up until Jane Austen's time, since this was her inheritance.

A brief history of names

Two mechanisms inform the common stock of English Christian names at any given period. The first is the accretion of whole new sets of names at various points in our history. Like the English language itself, the naming system has welcomed and acclimatised contributions from a variety of sources. A glance through any babies' name book will show that some are Hebrew, some Germanic, some Greek, some literary inventions, and so forth. A name's origins (and original meaning, which is all that most of these books are concerned with) are, however, of much less significance to the choosers of names - parents and authors - than the operation of the second mechanism: the cyclical rise and fall of names on the social scale.

Typically, a name or set of names will be taken up at the top of the social hierarchy, being found alien, even absurd, by the majority. Eventually, through familiarity, it will become acceptable to a broad range of people; and by the time it has percolated to the very base of the pyramid, it will have long been shunned by the trend-setters, who are now looking elsewhere. Elsewhere might be a new set of imports, or more likely the revival of an old set of names. When sufficient time has elapsed since the last (usually comical) low-class bearers of a name have died and been forgotten, the name becomes eligible for revival at the top. (Think Emily, Benjamin and Rebecca thirty years ago, or Jack, Freddy and Daisy now. My daughter tells me Wilf and Archie are coming in for babies of her acquaintance. What next - Ivy? Bertha? Enid? Albert? Ernest? The unthinkable will become the fashionable one day.)

Like any aspect of life subject to the whims of choice, and therefore of fashion, the process is always accelerating. The slippage that now takes place in a generation used to take a century, or several centuries, and was often retarded by the custom of passing on family names. There are exceptions to this fashionable cycle, of course, and some names have remained a minority choice, cropping up now and then apparently at random. Others are timeless, having lasted now for a thousand years in more or less unbroken popularity - William, for example.

The English name-stock has been much influenced by royalty. Many of our most popular female names came to us first by marriage among the royal houses of Europe, from Anne and Eleanor in the Middle Ages to Charlotte and Sophia in the Georgian period. There were few English men named Charles or George until the first kings of these names made them familiar, in the seventeenth and eighteenth centuries respectively. Royal usage preserved pre-Conquest names that might otherwise have died out, like Edward and Arthur, and in Tudor times brought names like Jane and Elizabeth into prominence. The curious thing is that throughout British history the two groups in society whose Christian names were heard and used by all were royalty - and the lowliest of servants.

> *They say his name is Henry. A proof of how unequally the gifts of Fortune are bestowed - I have seen many a John & Thomas much more agreable.*
> **Letters**

English nomenclature begins with the Old English system of names created by combining two elements from a stock of special naming words. Often one component would be taken from the father's name and joined to one that was different. (Hence Edred, Ethelred, Ethelbert, Egbert and so forth.) Very few of these names survived the Conquest, though favoured ones were revived after Jane Austen's time, during the Victorians' passion for antiquarianism. Old English names which *did* survive to be passed down the centuries with unbroken (though varying degrees of) usage into Jane Austen's day, include Edward, Edmund and Arthur, all of which she favoured, as we shall see. Emma, another favourite with her, is one of the few lapsed Old English names to be revived as early as the eighteenth century, doubtless because it chimed well with the Georgian vogue for a-endings.

The Norman Conquest swept away all but the remnants of this system and brought in not only a whole new set of names, such as William, Walter, Richard and Robert, but the concept of a limited stock of *fixed* names, to be drawn on by everybody. In the 12th and 13th centuries the increasing power of the church to influence every aspect of life was reflected in the frequent choice of saints' names, both scriptural (i.e. found in the Bible) and early Christian. Catherine was first recorded in England in 1189, Mary in 1203, and Anne in 1218. While John appears once in the Domesday Book, by the end of the 13th century, 25% of boys were being christened John. With 38% of men sharing just five Christian names, of necessity nicknames and identifiers came into use, from which evolved hereditary surnames. (John the Shepherd, John down the Lane, John the son of Robin - itself a pet form of Robert…)

Many surnames in fact derive from Christian names, both male and female. A good indicator of how widespread a name was in the Middle Ages is how many surnames have been formed from it, or from its diminutives and nicknames. Jane Austen's own surname derives from Augustine, founder of Canterbury Cathedral, and is found predominantly in Kent. Surnames derived from first names in the novels include Bennet, descended from Benedict, Tilney, from Matilda, and Watson, from Walter.

After the Reformation the names of the non-scriptural saints fell into disgrace and disuse, names like Basil, Stephen, Nicholas, Christopher, Agnes, and Barbara. Helped by their royal connections, Margaret and Catherine survived the cull, though with diminished popularity. To remain religious without being idolatrous, parents turned to the Old Testament for inspiration. A few Old Testament names had long been familiar to the English people from the mystery plays, but with the vernacular Bible many more became available. Names like Daniel, Benjamin, Isaac, Samuel, Judith, Sarah and Rebecca now began their long run of widespread usage. The Puritans distinguished themselves by choosing some of the less easily assimilated Old Testament names (Ezekiel, Obadiah) together with a name-stock of their own invention, based on moral qualities (Chastity, Praise-God), but this was a short-lived phase.

With the Enlightenment came an interest in Classical literature and a growing taste for names such as Diana, Julia, Penelope, Augustus / Augusta and Octavius / Octavia. This was the first time that names had broken free from religion to any large degree for six centuries and marked a definite shift to which Jane Austen was heir.

Strangely, Jane Austen's own sister's name, Cassandra, a pagan name if ever there was one, had been in use in England since the Middle Ages, owing to the popularity even then of the romanticised story of Troy. It was never very common, however, those who chose it seeming to do so *despite* the unpleasant aspects of the original Cassandra's story and the unchristian nature of the name. It came into Jane Austen's family in the 1720s, when the Duke of Chandos married as his second wife Cassandra Willoughby. The Duke's sister, Mary Brydges, married Theophilus Leigh, Jane Austen's great-grandfather, and many of their descendants - right up to our own times - were and are named Cassandra. Charlotte Mary Yonge, in her *History of Christian Names* of 1863, writes "Cassandra appears in Essex in 1560, and is still not forgotten in Hants families," by which I feel she must mean the Austens. Yonge was a Hampshire woman herself.

> *The name of Rachael is more than I can bear.*
>
> **Letters**

Names in Jane Austen's time

Perhaps because religion was taken more quietly in the eighteenth century, the Old Testament names, though still familiar in Jane Austen's lifetime, were beginning to decline in popularity, especially among the upper echelons of society. This was a great impoverishment of the name-stock, particularly for men. Between 1750 and 1799, when most of the people Jane Austen knew were born and named, 20% of boys christened in England were William, 19% John and 16% Thomas, with Edward, Richard, Robert, Charles, Henry and James filling up most of the rest. No wonder then that so many of her male characters go by these names. Nevertheless, there were other names among her own gentlemen acquaintance with which she could have varied her repertoire, but chose not to do so: David, Gilbert, Guy, Hugh, Michael, Nicholas, Peter and Ralph were wholly rejected for her mature fiction, though they would seem to be the common names of common life that she so favoured.

Similarly with girls in the same period: 24% were given the name of Mary, 19% Elizabeth and 14% Anne, and this preponderance is reflected both in Jane Austen's acquaintance and in her fiction. However, there was a greater variety of names for girls in circulation. To suit the Classical taste of the age, latinate forms of existing girls' names were found or adopted from literature: Anna, Maria, Cecilia and Isabella. Many completely new names were created by feminising male names, such as Henrietta, Louisa and Georgiana with the favoured a-ending, or Harriet, Caroline and Charlotte.

It is the latinate names that Jane Austen tends to use in her fiction for pretentious or shallow young women: we have only to think of Isabella and Maria Thorpe, Louisa Hurst, Lydia Bennet, Maria Lucas, Maria and Julia Bertram, Augusta Elton and Selina Suckling to appreciate the pattern. Better-disposed, but still without a great deal of depth, are Isabella Knightley and Henrietta and Louisa Musgrove. With very few exceptions, most notably Emma Woodhouse and Emma Watson, it would seem that if a young woman's first name end in the letter a, we can expect her to have little or none of her author's approval. But the only outright comment in the novels comes in the good-humoured perplexity of Admiral Croft: "I wish young ladies did not have such a number of fine christian names. I would never be out, if they were all Sophys, or something of that sort."

As we have seen, it was almost *de rigueur* for novelists of the period to invent for their heroines polysyllabic names. The habit had perhaps begun with Fielding (who had caught it from the playwrights) when he invented the name Pamela for his heroine. (It is hard to appreciate now how radical Charlotte Brontë was being, even a generation after Jane Austen had quietly led the way, in naming *her* heroine plain Jane.) Not that it was only authors who were inventive. Among her own real-life acquaintance, Jane Austen knew a Christiana, Florentina, Honoria, Marianna and Margaretta. It seemed the 'a' could be added to almost anything to make a female name.

Fanny Burney, while conforming to expectations by employing the names Evelina, Cecilia, Camilla and Indiana for the favoured female characters in her novels, also had some fun with the fashion. In her play *A Busy Day* (1801), the vulgar but would-be-fashionable young lady Miss Watts is named Margaret, her sister Elizabeth or Eliza. However, Miss Watts wants them to be known as Margarella and Eliziana. Their hopeless parents *will* keep calling them Peg and Bet… and when scolded by their daughter, they get into a muddle and come out with 'Peggarelly' and 'Elizinenny'.

The diminutives that come so easily to the lips of Mr and Mrs Watts were increasingly being seen as vulgar in Jane Austen's lifetime. For most of the seventeenth and eighteenth centuries, even high-born ladies had been known by the contractions of their names: Betty (much more often than Lizzy), Kitty, Peggy, Nanny, Sally, Molly, Polly, Jenny, Patty, Hetty, Nelly, Biddy, Dolly and Fanny for Elizabeth, Catherine, Margaret, Anne, Sarah, Mary, Mary Anne, Jane, Martha, Hester (or Henrietta), Eleanor, Bridget, Dorothy and Frances respectively. These diminutives or pet forms show an astonishing conformity to pattern. There seems no logical reason why Mary should become Molly and Martha become Patty - but they did. As for Anne and Jane, it was not a question of shortening them, so diminutive or contraction is hardly the word - only pet form will do. It was natural, of course, to call children by these pet forms, but by the time Jane Austen was publishing, only Fanny was still acceptable as a name for a woman of the gentry. (But Mr Price manages to vulgarise even that, by calling his daughter Fan - shades of Mr and Mrs Watts!) The rest of the y-ending names had become maidservant names and Jane Austen finds it most natural, when naming a maidservant (particularly of a humble household) to choose Sally, Nanny, Betty or Patty.

Here it might be worth remarking that when Jane Austen was born, in 1775, her father, in writing to announce the joyful news to relatives, announces her name thus: "She is to be Jenny". No mention anywhere in the letter of 'Jane' - by which name she was certainly christened. It would seem that very soon after Jane Austen's birth the diminutive began to seem dated and inferior, and she was never known by it, though her wealthy and snobbish aunt Jane Leigh Perrot was called Jenny all her life by her husband: evidence of the generational change. Only old ladies, in Jane Austen's novels, share these humble names with servants.

A poem by Charles Lamb, written in 1809, the year that Jane Austen moved to Chawton and began her second great period of creativity, purports to come from a young girl invited to choose a name for her new sister:

Now I wonder what would please her,
Charlotte, Julia or Louisa?
Ann and Mary, they're too common
Joan's too formal for a woman:
Jane's a prettier name beside;
But we had a Jane that died.
They would say, if 'twas Rebecca
That she was a little Quaker.
Edith's pretty, but that looks
Better in old English books.
Ellen's left off long ago:

Blanche is out of fashion now.
None that I have named as yet
Are so good as Margaret.
Emily is neat and fine.
What do you think of Caroline?

Having reached Jane Austen's own time, and established the social status of various categories of names at the time she was writing, we need take the story of names no further forward, except to note two things. One is that in reaction to the names of the period before them, and in the relentless cycle of fashion, the Victorians despised the a-ending. To them it was formal and artificial, on a par with the Georgian architecture which they also despised. Charlotte Mary Young, writing in 1863, has many cutting things to say about such names, even deploring her own first name as being "a clumsy feminisation of an essentially masculine name". She was much more comfortable with her middle name, and welcomed the return of what she regards as simple honest names like Ellen, Lucy and Amy. This change for the better, as she sees it, she cites as beginning after the second decade of the nineteenth century - in other words, immediately after Jane Austen's death - and attributes it to the influence on the literate classes of "the chivalrous school of Scott, and the simplicity upheld by Wordsworth".

A good example of the changing fashion is Philadelphia versus Phyllis. The former was the name of Jane Austen's aunt and a cousin, and is mentioned twice by Yonge, both times with great disfavour. Having stated that the city of Philadelphia (which of course means brotherly love) was mentioned in the Apocalypse, and that the Quaker William Penn took it for the capital of his new colony, she adds, "Less happily, Philadelphia has even been used among English women, apparently desirous of a large mouthful of name." Regarding Phyllis, which is found in the *dramatis personae* of Arcadian literature and in Milton's "neat-handed Phyllis" as a country maid, she tells us that by mid-nineteenth century it has become a popular name in England, "used at first as a contraction of the formidable Philadelphia, and, in process of time, was herself given as a baptismal name; a happy change".

The second point to note is that there was a massive expansion in the national name-stock as names were drawn into regular usage from the distant past, from the Celtic fringes, and indeed from a variety of sources, in the later nineteenth and twentieth centuries. We have as part of our mental furniture hundreds of names that were unavailable to Jane Austen. It is no part of the present work to describe these intervening fashions. The extraordinary thing is that in 1939, when the Ethels and Ednas, Maureens and Mavises, Sheilas and Sylvias and a myriad others had come and gone, the top ten girls' names as taken from the birth announcements in *The Times* were precisely those used over and over again by Jane Austen: Anne, Mary, Elizabeth, Jane, Susan, Margaret, Sarah, Caroline, Penelope and Frances.

There were only 4 dances, & it went to my heart that the Miss Lances (one of them too named Emma!) should have partners for only two.

Letters

Naming patterns and practices

The custom which is so prevalent both in Jane Austen's novels and among her acquaintance, of naming firstborn sons and daughters after their parents, with subsequent children named for grandparents, aunts and uncles etc, might seem to go back to time immemorial, but had taken root among the gentry generally only about the beginning of the 17th century. Since one of the pleasures of having a baby is choosing its name, this seems a cruel imposition on the rights of parents. I always feel sorry for the John Knightleys, who have had five children without being able to choose an original name for one of them. And then I wonder about the George Knightleys - will they duplicate all the same names, or strike out afresh? And if the latter, will they be glad to do so or sorry?

Children were frequently named for godparents, though when a limited number of names revolved in a community, it is hard to know whether the godparents were chosen to fit the preferred name or *vice versa*. In a society where 'getting on' was so dependent on inheritance and influence, it is not surprising to find children named after wealthy relatives and patrons. The Austens themselves gave their first son not his father's name but that of his rich uncle James Leigh Perrot. In a novel which Jane Austen mentions in *Emma*, *The Vicar of Wakefield* (1765), Oliver Goldsmith writes, "Our eldest son was called George, after his uncle, who left us ten thousand pounds"

Squire Allworthy, in Fielding's novel *Tom Jones*, in standing godfather to the foundling, automatically gives him his own name of Thomas. He is conferring his protection and favour with his name. In *Mansfield Park*, the occasion of Mrs Price's seeking reconciliation with her rich relations is that she is expecting her ninth child and "imploring their countenance as sponsors". The child must be Tom - whom Fanny remembers nursing as a baby before her departure from Portsmouth. Sir Thomas Bertram has evidently stood godfather to the unseen child. Then comes Charles, born after Fanny's departure and possibly called after Mr Norris? - and Betsey, whose godmother we know is Mrs Norris.

The medieval practice of inviting a godparent freely to *choose* the child's name had not entirely died out. The Vicar of Wakefield, after explaining that his eldest daughter was named Olivia because his wife had been reading romances, continues, "In less than another year we had another daughter, but a rich relation taking a fancy to stand godmother, the girl was, by her directions, called Sophia, so that we had two romantic names in the family, but I solemnly protest I had no hand in it."

Oliver Goldsmith was evidently interested in the subject of Christian names, since elsewhere in his work he mocks the fashion of giving children more than one name in the character of Miss Carolina Wilhelmina Amelia Skeggs. This was certainly a new phenomenon. In 1605, in the first study of English Christian names, Camden cites James I and his son as being the only people he has ever heard of with two Christian names. Charles I's Queen Henrietta Maria (Henriette Marie in her native French, named for her two parents), by being always known by her double name, familiarised the concept to the British people. An illegitimate child of Charles II born in 1650 was given the names Charlotte Jemima Henrietta Maria. It will be seen that the concurrent fashions for giving more than one name, for making female names out of male, and for naming children after family members or influential connections, were highly inter-related. They were all the consequence of a propertied and patriarchal society.

The children of George III, born in the 1760s and 70s, had a very unequal number of names, being, in order of birth: George Augustus Frederick; Frederick; William Henry; Charlotte Augusta Matilda; Edward Augustus; Augusta Sophia; Elizabeth; Ernest Augustus; Augustus Frederick; Adolphus Frederick; Mary; Sophia; Octavius; Alfred and Amelia. Four Augustuses, two Augustas, four Fredericks and two Sophias suggest a dearth of imagination, as does the gradual petering out in number of names. The opposite pattern operated in the Austen family, born in the same decades. The first three children were given just one name, the next three two names each, then one again (Jane herself) and then two. (James; George; Edward; Henry Thomas; Cassandra Elizabeth; Francis William; Jane; Charles John.) I always feel sorry that Jane was given no second name; the imbalance between her one syllable and her sister Cassandra's seven pains me. Could not Jane have been Jane Catherine, after the wife of the family benefactor, Mrs Knight, or Jane Philadelphia (notwithstanding C.M. Yonge), after her aunt?

Giving each child two names became a commonplace in the generation of Austens after Jane, whereas it had been unheard of among her mother and father's generation. There were even instances of three names being given within the Austen family, though this was unusual enough to cause remark. James Austen's first daughter was named Jane Anna Elizabeth, the first name not so much for his sister as for the child's grandmother, who had been Lady Jane Bertie, the daughter of a duke. James's second daughter, by his second wife, was given the Christian names Caroline Mary Craven. Their cousin Fanny (Frances Catherine Austen, later Knight) wrote to her old governess, in July 1805, 'We have had my Grandmama Austen, & two Aunts here for the last six weeks, & my cousin Anna, she has just got another little Sister, who, determined not to be outdone by her in names, has likewise 3, they are Caroline, Mary, Craven!' The Mary was for her mother, Craven for *her* mother's maiden name, and Caroline probably because the prized ancestor, Lord Craven, had been Governor of Carolina.

Fanny herself, though the first child, was named not for her mother but for her grandmother, Fanny, Lady Bridges, and the wealthy and childless Mrs Catherine Knight. One of Fanny's own sisters, Cassandra Jane, had two names like herself, the others, Elizabeth, Marianne and Louisa, just one. (It is Elizabeth and Marianne who appear on the cover of this book.) Jane Austen was godmother to two of her nieces: the Louisa mentioned above, who strangely did *not* get her name; and Charles's daughter Harriet Jane, named for an aunt on each side of the family.

One odd naming practice within the larger family circle concerned Fanny's maternal uncles, who all (except one) had the same first name. Fanny's grandfather Sir Brook Bridges named his sons Brook, Brook William, Brook Henry, Charles, Brook Edward, Brook John and Brook George. Fanny's own sixth brother was Brook John - the only one of her brothers to have two names.

In the fiction, there are only two characters of whom we are told they have two Christian names apiece: William Walter Elliot (the middle name a dynastic one, the name of his great-grandfather and later members of the family) and Frederica Susanna Vernon, named for her two parents, Lady Susan and Frederic Vernon. Unlike Goldsmith, Jane Austen refrained from bestowing a string of names on any of her more pretentious characters. But who is to say that Selina and Augusta Hawkins do not have middle names? From being a way of honouring (or currying favour with) more than one influential family connection for the upper classes, the fashion for multiple names in slipping down the social scale became for the bourgeoisie just that: a fashion, charming or affected according to the point of view. This was the fashion that the Brontë sisters mocked when they dubbed one of their father's handsome young curates "Miss Celia Amelia".

By contrast, at the other end of the social spectrum female names were shrinking. Among the uneducated classes, Betty, Peggy, Sally and so forth were increasingly becoming baptismal names in their own right. In a survey of 200 English parish registers of 1700, there are 441 Elizabeths to just one Betty; one hundred years later, the figures were 335 to 82. A like increase applies to the other pet forms. It is thought that the lower orders had long presented their girls for baptism by these names, but that clergymen had formalised the names in the register; now, more and more, they were accepting the name the parents spoke. It would appear that having now been almost totally discarded by the gentry, these diminutives had become so much the property of the lower orders that they were increasingly divorced from the names from which they sprang. Perhaps some clergymen actually liked to see, in names as in other facets of life, "the distinction of rank preserved" - as Lady Catherine de Bourgh would say.

The only merit it could have, was in the name of Caleb,
which has an honest, unpretending sound.
Letters

THE USE OF CHRISTIAN NAMES

To use a person's Christian name was a mark of intimacy. Well-bred people with feelings of delicacy towards others did not presume on this intimacy until it was clear that an acquaintance was becoming a real friendship. Most acquaintance, of course, never progressed this far, and people would remain on formal terms for as long as they knew each other. Isabella Thorpe has neither delicacy nor good breeding; she rushes the inexperienced Catherine Morland into an intimacy that has no foundation in real feeling:

> The progress of the friendship between Catherine and Isabella was as quick as its beginning had been warm, and they passed so rapidly through every gradation of increasing tenderness that there was shortly no fresh proof of it to be given to their friends or themselves. They called each other by their Christian name…

In contrast, the friendship between Catherine and Eleanor Tilney progresses with due decorum but is enduring, based on secure knowledge of one another's characters and values. Although we may not realise it until we search the text, it is not until the very night of the General's barbarously turning Catherine out of doors that we hear Eleanor and Catherine use each other's Christian names.

Mary Crawford, who combines good breeding with warmth of heart, speaks (or rather, writes) of "stumbling at *Miss Price* for at least the last six weeks" when she has been longing to address Fanny by her first name. The desire for friendship, of course, is not reciprocated, and Fanny stubbornly keeps her at a distance by continuing to use the term 'Miss Crawford' in her reply note, in speech and even in her thoughts. Mary does not take the hint but continues to address Fanny by her first name many times. Perhaps she supposes that it is only Fanny's humility which keeps her from using her own first name. In fact, the formal etiquette of the day is a gift to Fanny, enabling her to be as unfriendly as her heart dictates, yet remain irreproachably correct.

It was even harder for a man to break through the Christian name barrier, and Henry Crawford - who thinks he has won the right by honourably proposing marriage to Fanny - offends her mightily by so doing. It comes out in the middle of a long address, all of which she would rather not hear:

> "- Yes, dearest, sweetest Fanny - Nay - (seeing her draw back displeased) forgive me. Perhaps I have as yet no right - but by what other name can I call you? Do you suppose you are ever present to my imagination under any other? No, it is 'Fanny' that I think of all day, and dream of all night. - You have given the name a reality of sweetness, that nothing else can now be descriptive of you."
>
> Fanny could hardly have kept her seat any longer...

As it is more insulting for a man to assume intimacy against a woman's wishes, unlike his sister Henry does not dare to call Fanny by her first name again - at least to her face. On the only two further occasions on which they meet, at Portsmouth, he avoids addressing her by any name at all.

The use by a man of a woman's Christian name, unless they are family connections, could normally only happen after a successful proposal. So when Elinor Dashwood hears Willoughby "addressing her sister by her Christian name alone", that is, without the 'Miss' that should proceed a younger sister's Christian name, "she instantly saw an intimacy so decided, a meaning so direct, as marked a perfect agreement between them. From that moment she doubted not of their being engaged to each other." Of course, they are not, and Marianne has erred in allowing the familiarity.

After his engagement is known, Frank Churchill writes a long letter to his stepmother Mrs Weston, in which he includes some censure of Mrs Elton's treatment of Jane Fairfax. "'Jane', indeed!" he writes. "You will observe that I have not yet indulged myself in calling her by that name, even to you. Think, then, what I must have endured in hearing it bandied between the Eltons with all the vulgarity of needless repetition, and all the insolence of imaginary superiority."

Like Isabella Thorpe, Mrs Elton has no delicacy of character to restrain her tongue. Calling Jane Fairfax 'Jane' to her face is patronising, and referring to her as 'Jane Fairfax' instead of 'Miss Fairfax' is underbred. "Let me not suppose that she dares go about, Emma Woodhouse-ing me!" thinks Emma. Yet Emma herself calls her 'little friend' Harriet, never 'Miss Smith'. This is just as patronising, though her social position gives Emma slightly more right to patronise than Mrs Elton. It certainly never purports to be a friendship of equals, of mutual confidence. Harriet herself always uses the respectful 'Miss Woodhouse' of someone addressing a superior. It is evidently not the case that Harriet has invited Emma to call her by her first name, rather that Emma assumes the right. Similarly, Fanny Price calls her cousin Maria 'Miss Bertram' while Maria calls her 'Fanny'. But then, Mrs Norris calls Lady Bertram 'Lady Bertram', while her ladyship calls Mrs Norris 'sister'. And Mary Crawford calls *her* married sister 'Mrs Grant', while being addressed as 'Mary' herself. Evidently marriage and seniority played a part as well as social status.

While Mr Woodhouse calls Mr Knightley 'Mr Knightley', the latter calls Mr Woodhouse 'sir'. Mrs Weston does not call or refer to her former pupil as Isabella, but by her married name. Will she cease to call Emma 'Emma' once she is married? Mr Weston, by marrying her governess, seems to have won the right to call Emma by her first name, which one would have thought she might have resented. No other of their neighbours takes this liberty. When did he begin this practice - on becoming engaged to Miss Taylor, or only on marriage?

Emma is also indignant that Mrs Elton refers to Mr Knightley as Knightley. Here is a major change from the earlier novels. In *Sense and Sensibility*, *Pride and Prejudice* and the juvenilia, young men are commonly referred to by their surnames only. There is much talk of Bingley, Darcy, Wickham and Willoughby, even by the heroines, though in speaking *to* these men they usually - not invariably - give them the title Mr. Perhaps the most important thing to note is that the *narrator* calls these men by their surnames, so that is how the reader thinks of them. Don't we speak among ourselves of Willoughby or Wickham without feeling we are being at all vulgar? Yet we would never speak of Churchill or Elliot.

This is another of those generational changes that show themselves between the late eighteenth century, when Jane Austen was growing up and writing her first three novels, and the early nineteenth century, when her three later novels were written. What is perhaps strange is that in revising *Sense and Sensibility* and *Pride and Prejudice* she did not bring this aspect of manners up to date. In publishing terms, only three years separate Lady Catherine de Bourgh calling her nephews 'Darcy' and 'Fitzwilliam' with authorial impunity and Mrs Elton being so severely castigated for saying 'Knightley'.

That Jane Austen herself used the surname only for young men is proved by her letters. A childhood friend - a pupil of her father's the same age as herself - is always referred to by her as 'Buller': no Christian name, no Mr (except on one occasion when she seems to be quoting a servant). Even by the time of *Emma*, however, it was evidently not vulgar for men to use the surname only: in conversation with Mrs Weston, Mr Knightley, model of good breeding, refers to her husband as 'Weston', while she uses the term 'Mr Weston'.

"It amuses me to hear John Bridges talk of 'Frank'," Jane Austen writes in a letter, evidently struck by the use of the Christian name by one only related by marriage to the family. So much are the young men in the novels identified with their surnames that it is these only which awake romantic feelings in female breasts. Marianne never sighs over the Christian name John, or Jane Bennet over Charles. Yet Edward Ferrars is always thought of and usually addressed as Edward within the Dashwood family. This is strange, because he is in the same relation to the Dashwoods as Mr Knightley is to Emma - a brother-in-law, but a much newer acquaintance - yet Emma famously cannot imagine calling her husband 'George'. Caroline Bingley, in speaking to her sister, refers to her brother-in-law as 'Mr Hurst'. Even Fanny Price, brought up with Edmund, never actually addresses him by his first name, much though she loves it and thinks about it, but always as 'cousin'.

Indeed, few husbands and wives are heard addressing each other by their first names. Oddly, in the famous second chapter of *Sense and*

Sensibility, where John and Fanny Dashwood are debating how he should help his sisters, he calls his wife 'My dear Fanny' while she calls him 'My dear Mr Dashwood'. Similarly, Jane Austen's aunt, Jane Leigh Perrot, always referred to her husband in speech and writing as 'Perrot', though he addresses her, in letters at least, as 'My dear Jenny'. Charles and Mary Musgrove use each other's first names, and Mr Parker of *Sanditon* calls his wife Mary. Harriet Smith is thrilled by Mr Elton openly calling his bride Augusta. These of course are all young couples. Otherwise, we hear Mrs Bennet call her husband 'Mr Bennet', Lady Bertram call hers 'Sir Thomas', and Mrs Croft call hers 'my dear admiral'. Mrs Musgrove does not refer to her daughter-in-law as Mary, but as 'Mrs Charles'.

Children sometimes call their parents 'Sir' and 'Madam', sometimes 'Papa' and 'Mamma'. Aunts are known just as 'Aunt' (e.g. Miss Bates) unless there is more than one of them, in which case they are 'Aunt Bertram' and 'Aunt Norris'. No Aunt Hetty or Aunt Maria - yet Jane Austen and her sister seem to have been known to their nephews and nieces as Aunt Jane and Aunt Cassandra.

Where there is more than one unmarried sister in a family, the elder or eldest is correctly addressed or referred to as Miss Bennet, Miss Bertram, etc, the younger ones as Miss Elizabeth Bennet, Miss Julia Bertram, etc. (How many readers pick up that Mrs Norris is the eldest of the three sisters, which is why her Christian name is not given? Had Lady Bertram been not only the first to marry but the eldest, the first words of *Mansfield Park* would have been 'About thirty years ago, Miss Ward, of Huntingdon...') Jane Austen once had occasion to correct - tactfully, we may be sure - a young man who referred to her sister as Miss Cassandra, taking her as the younger. Cassandra would have heard her first name spoken much less frequently than Jane. Outside the family she was never called by her first name, being an unmarried elder (or only) sister all her life - until the time came, when her old mother died and she was left alone, the head of a household of one, that she assumed the title of Mrs Austen - or at least asked to be addressed that way in correspondence.

The first names of younger sisters were used chiefly when both are present or in conversation when there could be any ambiguity. When Elizabeth stays in Kent or Derbyshire without Jane she is usually elevated to 'Miss Bennet', particularly by those who do not know the rest of the family, like Lady Catherine de Bourgh. So too with younger brothers - Mary Crawford, who is not partial to the idea of younger brothers, deplores the return of Tom Bertram, thereby relegating his brother to 'Mr Edmund Bertram' from simply 'Mr Bertram'. Of course, sons also have to be distinguished from fathers, and Tom can only be Mr Bertram because his father is Sir Thomas. In contrast, Frank Churchill is properly given his Christian name to distinguish him from Mr Churchill - his uncle.

The daughters of Earls are known, from birth, as Lady, Christian name, surname - e.g. Lady Marianne Leven, a child acquaintance of Jane Austen. On marriage, unless elevated to a yet higher rank, they keep their title and change only the surname, even when marrying a commoner. Thus Lady Anne Darcy is married to plain Mr Darcy, and their son has no title. Lady Susan Vernon is likewise evidently the daughter of an Earl. The daughters of baronets and knights have no title (Miss Elliot, Miss Anne Elliot) and their wives do not use the Christian name in their title: Lady Elliot, Lady Russell. Younger sons of Earls are also correctly known by their Christian names all their lives: Lord David Cecil, Lord Peter Wimsey. (I have been obliged to look elsewhere for my examples, since Jane Austen has no male characters of this rank. She does have the occasional Honourable, however, such as the Hon. John Yates, the younger son of a Lord.)

The Christian name alone was used for many male servants. Among Jane Austen's fictional manservants are Thomas, John, Stephen, William and Robert, the single name seeming to denote a man in the personal service of his master or mistress, who could be called on to do anything required. Upper servants, or those with a special role, were usually known by their surnames alone: Serle the butler, Wilcox the coachman, Mackenzie the gardener. But in other novels there is James the coachman and Andrew the gardener, so different rules must have applied in different households. James and Andrew are not young, James being a father of a girl old enough to go out into service, and Andrew actually being referred to as 'old Andrew', so it is not their youth that determines their style, as might have been the case at Chawton Cottage. Here the Austens' first manservant was Thomas; he was replaced by Browning; and when *he* left, by William, who was only a 'lad'. Whatever the rationale or particular circumstances, the point is that it was one name or another. Only tradesmen and skilled labouring men with a sturdy independence are recognised as such by their having two names always used together: William Larkins, Christopher Jackson, Jack Stokes. Even the tenant farmer falls into this category: Mr Knightley always speaks of 'Robert Martin', not 'Mr Martin' or 'Martin'.

With females, there was a similar division was between the ordinary maidservant - Sally, Rebecca - and the specialised and probably older servant, known by her surname and almost always dignified with the courtesy title Mrs (whether married or not): Mrs Hodges, Mrs Whitaker. Lady Bertram refers to her lady's maid as 'Chapman', though the narrator calls her Mrs Chapman - similarly with the housekeeper at Longbourn, whom Mrs Bennet calls 'Hill'.

Finally there is the convention by which people signed their names in correspondence. It comes as a surprise to find Jane Austen signing her letters even to a beloved sister as either 'JA', or 'J Austen', the latter also used when writing to nieces. Long after her death when a few people were beginning to seek relics, her brother Frank, longest-lived of all the family, was unable to find an autograph of her complete name among the papers in his possession. "She scarcely ever wrote her Christian name at full length," he told the supplicant, "except when writing to some of her most intimate friends, when she did not use her sirname *[sic]*." In fact, there is no extant letter signing herself just Jane, even to intimate family or friends, and the only ones signed 'Jane Austen' are to her publisher. Of course, her name did not appear on her books in her lifetime, and the first time it was seen in print was in Henry Austen's very brief account of her life, the *Biographical Notice* attached to the posthumously published *Northanger Abbey* and *Persuasion*.

Jane Austen's feeling for names

The fact that Jane Austen recycles the same limited number of names and tends to favour conservative names for the majority of her characters, has perhaps concealed what was actually a lively interest in the subject on her part. We should hardly be surprised - writers relish words, and names are just especially hallowed words. It would be a strange writer who was *not* sensitive to names, each with its sounds and associations capable of arousing a variety of emotions.

The first inkling of the interest that she took in the subject comes in the playful entries she made on the specimen pages of her father's parish register of marriages when she was about fifteen. She tried out a selection of husbands for herself, beginning with 'Henry Frederic Howard Fitzwilliam', moving on to 'Edmund Arthur William Mortimer', and finally plain 'Jack Smith'. If we discount this last as a pure joke, we can discern a taste for a certain kind of name - romantic, medieval, aristocratic - that was to remain with her all her life. No fewer than five of her heroes are foreshadowed in the names of these two imaginary lovers, if we include the Mr Howard (Christian name unspecified) who was, according to family tradition - well supported by indications in the text - to be the hero of the unfinished fragment *The Watsons*.

Frederick (with or without the k), Edmund and Arthur carried echoes from the Middle Ages, and would grow in popularity with the nineteenth century. Jane Austen has no romantic Arthurs - rather the reverse, in Arthur Parker - and she may have been put off by its being used as the hero of his novel *Arthur Fitz-Albini* (1798) by Samuel Egerton Brydges, whom she knew and whose work she deplored. But nothing intervened to destroy her youthful preference for Frederick and Edmund, names bestowed on two of the heroes created more than twenty years after those parish register entries. Her affection for these names was remarkably enduring. In the novels, the warmest eulogy she gives to any name is to Edmund, name of "heroism and renown". "That must be Edmund," she wrote of a distant acquaintance in 1801, trying to distinguish one member of a family from another. That she had remembered there was an Edmund in the family suggests a retentive memory for names and an interest in that particular name.

Like many people from all periods she displays a pattern of liking names from the far past (Eleanor and Emma as well as the male names mentioned) but scorning those that were more recently outdated. Into the latter category fell the Old Testament names that were rapidly going out of fashion in her lifetime. The Sams and Sarahs tended to be reserved by her for rough and ready characters of rather low origin. Though her own paternal grandmother had been called Rebecca, in the novels it is fit only for a servant. In perhaps her strongest expression of dislike she once wrote to a niece, "The name of Rachael is as much as I can bear".

But to return to the names that she *did* like: Fitzwilliam Darcy is the only character in her novels who possesses a surname for his Christian name, despite Jane Austen knowing several men in real life named on this principle. Though the subject of this book is Christian names, it is worth remarking in this context that in choosing surnames for her heroes, she definitely had a penchant for those of the aristocracy: Wentworth, Ferrars, Tilney. (Mortimer was taken by Fanny Burney so was not available for Jane Austen to use.) Many aristocratic surnames were to become Christian names in the nineteenth century - that is, Christian names taken into the general stock, not confined to family connections. Howard and Vernon *(Lady Susan)* are two such aristocratic surnames that were to be common Christian names in the Victorian era and after, while Jane Austen herself made use of the mutation with Sidney, the hero of *Sanditon*. Surnames ending with y seem to have had an especial appeal for her: Darcy, Bingley, Tilney, Willoughby and Knightley were used by her for attractive men, and "Lesley *is* a noble name," she wrote to a niece who was writing a novel and had chosen the surname for a character. Jane Austen had in fact used it herself in one of her juvenile fragments, "Lesley Castle", where the family as well as their home is so named.

Henry was simply a favourite name, perhaps linked to the fact that Henry Austen was said to be her favourite brother. Of a new, and rather dull, acquaintance she wrote, "They say his name is Henry. A proof of how unequally the gifts of Fortune are bestowed - I have seen many a John & Thomas much more agreable *[sic]*." The Henrys in her novels tend to be witty and intelligent, while she uses John and Thomas for servants and gentry alike whenever a Christian name is wanted that means nothing. Mary Crawford seems to share her creator's disdain, speaking scathingly of "Mr John or Mr Thomas" to exemplify ordinariness.

Henry and Edward, which had never gone out of fashion, had been borne by a string of medieval monarchs. George too was a name of chivalry and renown, in his character as the patron saint of England. And we must not forget Reginald, who could be said to be the hero of *Lady Susan*, another medieval name. A survey of Jane Austen's heroes' names therefore reveals a common thread of aristocracy, romance, chivalry and medievalism, going right back to those youthful jottings in the parish register. She certainly allowed herself a little more leeway to be romantic with her heroes' than with her heroines' names. And as we have seen, this often extended to their surnames as well.

After Elinor and Marianne - names so euphonious that the novel they graced was to be eponymous, until the more perfect title of *Sense and Sensibility* was hit upon - Jane Austen confined herself mainly to what she herself called 'plain' names for her heroines. The exception is Emma - a name so well liked by her author that she could not resist not only naming the novel itself *Emma*, and opening the narrative with that very word, but introducing some word-play on the name into the text, by which it appears that Emma is 'perfection'. Moreover, this was the second time she had chosen the name for a heroine. Having abandoned *The Watsons* whose heroine is Emma, she recycled the name for a very differently circumstanced young woman, evidently being far too attached to the name to let it go. Besides this proof of attachment, her near-obsession with the name is clear from various remarks in her letters. The combination of Emma and Halifax struck her as almost too perfect, and upon hearing of the marriage of a young woman so named to a man with the rather bathetic name of Edward Bather, she wrote, "Wretch! - he does not deserve an Emma Halifax's maid Betty". She knew nothing of these people, having simply read the announcement in the papers, their names being enough to inspire her remark. In another letter she wrote, "There were only 4 dances, & it went to my heart that the Miss Lances (one of them too named Emma!) should have partners for only two".

"I admire the Sagacity & Taste of Charlotte Williams. Those large dark eyes always judge well. - I will compliment her, by naming a Heroine after her," she wrote in October 1813. But the name had to suit the character. She did not fulfil her pledge at the first opportunity - her next heroine was of course Emma Woodhouse, far too imaginative for a Charlotte, and then came Anne Elliot, whose unobtrusive, classic name is perfect for her: "She was only Anne". It was just over three years after the remark in her letter that she created Charlotte Heywood, well-judging heroine of *Sanditon*, begun in January 1817.

Cassandra Austen was the recipient of most of the remarks about names surviving in Jane Austen's letters, but in her later years there was another member of the family who shared her interest. This was her niece Fanny Austen, later Knight, seventeen years younger than Jane but when she grew up regarded by her as "almost another sister". Some of Jane's letters to Cassandra were written while the latter was staying at Godmersham, Fanny's home, so messages could be conveyed. "I am obliged to Fanny for the list of Mr Coleman's children, whose names I had not however quite forgot; the new one I am sure will be Caroline," she wrote in 1807. (The baby was in fact Elizabeth.) And again:

> I cannot yet satisfy Fanny as to Mrs Foote's baby's name, and I must not encourage her to expect a good one, as Captain Foote is a professed adversary of all but the plainest; he likes only Mary, Elizabeth, Anne etc. Our best chance is of 'Caroline' which in compliment to a sister seems the only exception.

Rather extraordinarily, this putative Caroline too was actually christened Elizabeth! But Jane Austen's guessing was third time lucky. This time it was she who was staying at Godmersham with Fanny and writing to Cassandra in London, "Fanny & I depend upon knowing what the child's name is to be, as soon as you can tell us. I guess Caroline." This occasion was the birth of Caroline Jane Tilson in October 1813.

In another letter, quoting a new acquaintance, Jane Austen writes, "*My* name is Diana - how does Fanny like it?" It evidently struck her as an unusual name, one that Fanny might relish. But aunt and niece did not always agree on names. The only evidence beyond her own writings of Jane Austen's taste in names comes in a letter which Fanny wrote to her ex-governess, Miss Chapman, in June 1809. Jane and Cassandra were both staying in Godmersham and had evidently heard of the birth of a baby called Robert. Fanny wrote, "Robert is too hideous to be born *[sic]* except by my two Aunts, Cassandra & Jane, who are very fond of both Robert & Susan!! did you ever hear of such a depraved taste? However it is not my fault." (I cannot help wondering whether the aunts were teasing Fanny - there is no charming Robert in the fiction.)

After all this evidence of Fanny's particular interest in names, I wondered what she herself would call her children. At the age of 24 Fanny married a widower with six children and, after five years of childless marriage, went on to have four daughters and five sons, all born in the 1820s and 30s. Five of the children were given family names: Fanny, Louisa, Edward, Richard and William. The other four reflect the taste for medieval names and were perhaps the kind Fanny (and her aunt?) had always wished for when she heard of babies being born: Matilda, Alice, Reginald and Herbert - who sound very much the Victorians they were to become.

Her aunt would not have approved of her choice of Richard. It seems to be the name for which she had the strongest irrational antipathy. "Mr Richard Harvey's match is to be put off, till he has got a better Christian name, of which he has great hopes," she wrote to Cassandra in 1796; and the first paragraph of *Northanger Abbey*, written not much later, continues what was perhaps a family joke, the heroine's father being described as "a very respectable man, though his name was Richard".

A similar but more explicable value-judgement seems to be made about the name Molly when she writes of an acquaintance, "I must feel for Miss Milles, though she *is* Molly". Mrs and Miss Milles, who were neighbours of Edward in Kent, were probably the partial inspiration for Mrs and Miss Bates in *Emma*, and it was the death of old Mrs Milles that occasioned Jane Austen's remark. She must have heard the mother call her daughter Molly, just as Mrs Bates calls hers Hetty. Molly and Hetty appeared inelegant names to those of Jane Austen's generation. In her novels, with great sureness of touch, she confines these old-fashioned diminutives to older women of unpretentious birth (see also Biddy Henshaw!) and younger ones of the serving classes, exemplifying the generational slide down the social scale of which she was so much aware. Her own family at various times employed servants called Molly, Sally and Jenny. Nanny, Patty and Betty are other servant names in the novels - and we have seen how even Emma Halifax's imaginary maid was designated Betty! It is one of those oddities of name fashion that while a y-ending made a male surname romantic and heroic, it made a female Christian name banal.

There is little in the letters to endorse the contempt for latinate girls' names which emerges from the novels with her consistent choice of such names for shallow, spoilt or affected young ladies. However, one comment in the letters is worth unpicking in this context. Her widowed friend Mrs Elizabeth Heathcote was being courted by a man who suddenly lost his fortune, through no fault of his own. Jane writes to Cassandra that if their friend "does not marry and comfort him now, I shall think she is quite a Maria & has no heart". The letters' most recent editor suggests that Jane Austen may have been making a specific reference to Maria Bertram (the letter was written in February 1813, as *Mansfield Park* was nearing completion). But to compare her respectable widowed friend with an adulteress would seem too gross an indelicacy for Jane Austen (to whom adultery was a grave offence), even in private correspondence. Besides, the circumstances were not at all alike: Maria Bertram does not give up a man for lack of fortune. It seems that Maria as a name simply conveyed to her the quality of heartlessness.

But that Emma was not the only a-ending name which she did not dislike is suggested by her remark on meeting a group of nondescript people in October 1813. Humorously searching to find something positive to say about one of them, she writes, "However Miss Chapman's name is Laura & she had a double flounce to her gown". Laura had been one of the two absurdly romantic heroines of her early burlesque, "Love and Freindship". Perhaps it was a name that she rather enjoyed, but felt impossible to use in fiction written for publication, especially after 1810. In that year was published *Self-Control,* by Mary Brunton, of which Jane Austen wrote, "I am looking over Self Control again, & my opinion is confirmed of its being an excellently-meant, elegantly-written Work, without anything of Nature or Probability in it. I declare I do not know whether Laura's passage down the American River, is not the most natural, possible, every-day thing she ever does."

It has been the purpose of this study to show that in nomenclature as in every other aspect of the novelist's art, Jane Austen had as much imagination and interest in the subject as her sister-novelists, but her sensitivity to the social nuances of names drew her in the opposite direction from most of them. For her, "Nature and Probability" were all-important, and she chose the names of her characters accordingly. As a result, her world is peopled with characters whose names rarely draw attention to themselves, but which add subtly to the depth and truthfulness of her portraits. The more we know about these names, the more fully we can enter into this world.

> *I cannot yet satisfy Fanny as to Mrs Foote's baby's name, and I must not encourage her to expect a good one, as Captain Foote is a professed adversary of all but the plainest; he likes only Mary, Elizabeth, Anne etc.*
>
> **Letters**

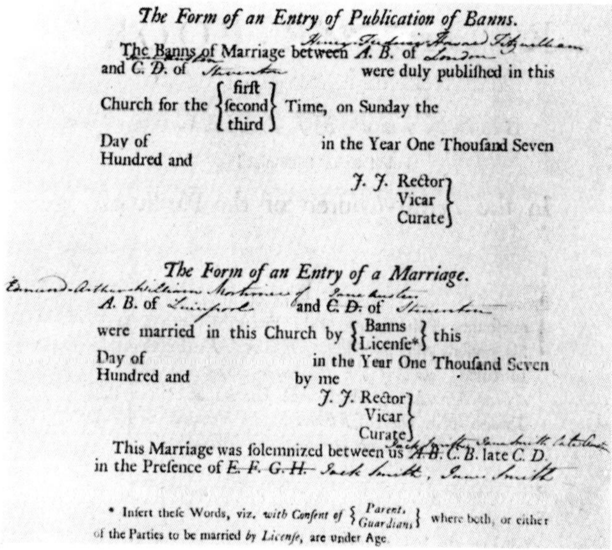

The Form of an Entry of Publication of Banns.

The Banns of Marriage between *A. B.* of and *C. D.* of were duly publiſhed in this Church for the {first / ſecond / third} Time, on Sunday the Day of in the Year One Thouſand Seven Hundred and

J. J. {Rector / Vicar / Curate}

The Form of an Entry of a Marriage.

A. B. of and *C. D.* of were married in this Church by {Banns / Licenſe*} this Day of in the Year One Thouſand Seven Hundred and by me

J. J. {Rector / Vicar / Curate}

This Marriage was ſolemnized between us *A. B.* *C. B.* late *C. D.* in the Preſence of *E. F.* *G. H.*

* Inſert theſe Words, viz. *with Conſent of* {*Parent*, / *Guardians*} where both, or either of the Parties to be married *by Licenſe*, are under Age.

Entries in Jane Austen's hand in the Steventon parish register of marriages

Names in the novels of Jane Austen:
an alphabetical index

Alice

Deriving from Old French and Old German, related to Adelaide, Alice was a popular name in medieval England. Like most such names, by the middle of the 17th century Alice was regarded as old-fashioned and rustic, fit only for servants and the like. It had to wait until the mid-19th century love affair with the Middle Ages for its revival as a fashionable name; the novelist Charlotte M Yonge called it 'a favourite fancy name' in 1863. It was the name of the real middle-class child who inspired Lewis Carroll to write *Alice in Wonderland*, the publication of which in 1865 spread the name's popularity. Writing before this revival, of course, Jane Austen used the name in her mature fiction only for a servant, **Alice** the maid of Eleanor Tilney in *Northanger Abbey*.

Alicia

In about the 12th century Alice was latinised into the alternative form, Alicia, picked up again in the 18th century with the vogue for such variants. It was used for the heroine of a novel known to Jane Austen, *Alicia de Lacey, an Historical Romance* by Mrs West, published in 1814. She herself gives the name to two well-bred women who would have been born perhaps mid-century: **Mrs Alicia Johnson** in *Lady Susan* and the non-speaking part **Lady Alicia**, acquaintance of Lady Russell, in *Persuasion*.

Andrew

Jane Austen may have given this name - her only use of it - to **Andrew** the gardener of the Parkers of *Sanditon*, because it was fashionable to have a Scottish gardener - her other example is Mackenzie of Kellynch in *Persuasion*. However, although Andrew is the patron saint of Scotland and strongly identified with that country, there were 637 churches in *England* dedicated to this saint - the fourth most frequent dedication.

Anna

A latinate and therefore perhaps more elegant form of the name Anne. Jane Austen gives the name only to **Anna Weston**, the baby born towards the end of *Emma*. She is named, with this slight variation in favour of the fashionable, after her mother Anne. It may be that Mrs Weston likes the echo of the name Emma in another four-lettered name ending with 'a'; or it may be that Jane Austen wishes to give a hint of the baby's being spoiled (which would hardly be surprising, given the age and fondness of her parents) by this more pretentious version of her sensible mother's name.

Annamaria

A combination of two latinate names, there is no doubting the affectation of this form, borne only by the spoiled child **Annamaria Middleton** in *Sense and Sensibility*. The only five-syllabled Christian name in the mature fiction, it surely indicates excessive petting and spoiling. Oddly, the same two names the other way round and reduced to a more reasonable three syllables occur in the same novel with Marianne Dashwood.

Anne

Deriving from the Hebrew Hannah, and arriving in Europe via royal marriages from princesses of Byzantium and Russia, Anne occurred first in England in the early 13th century. Becoming a royal name here too, its popularity grew steadily until by the beginning of the 17th century it was one of the commonest English names, remaining so for the next two centuries at least, and enjoying a further revival in the middle of the twentieth. Only its diminutives, Nan, Nanny and Nancy (qv) slipped down the social scale, Anne itself remaining timeless and classless. Jane Austen gives the name to her most perfect heroine, **Anne Elliot** of *Persuasion*, whose "sweetness of temper and elegance of mind must place her high with any people of merit", and for this character the name seems suitably unpretentious and elegant, as it does for **Mrs Weston**, *née* **Anne Taylor**, of *Emma*. Yet before this, Jane Austen had given the name to various less estimable characters: the sickly Anne de Burgh (named after her aunt, Lady Anne Darcy); and no fewer than four downright vulgarians. **Anne Thorpe** of Northanger Abbey is inferior even to her showy sister Isabella, whose friend Anne Mitchell is doubtless another of that ilk. **Anne Cox** of Emma and her elder unnamed sister are "the most vulgar girls in Highbury" according to Emma. And **Anne Steele** of *Sense and Sensibility*, known to her intimates as Nancy, is one of the few speaking-part characters to bear a lower-class diminutive, thus demonstrating her shaky hold on gentility.

Archibald

Always an uncommon name, and risked by Jane Austen only for the non-speaking **Sir Archibald Drew**, an acquaintance of Admiral Croft's in *Persuasion*.

Arthur

A name from medieval legend and Tudor royalty - Henry VII gave the name to his eldest son - it was not at all common until popularised by the Duke of Wellington (who was himself named after an Irish uncle). If Jane Austen meant anything at all in giving the name to **Arthur Parker** in *Sanditon* - written two years after the battle of Waterloo - it must have been in an ironic sense, as anybody less military could hardly be imagined. Her other Arthur is the non-speaking **Arthur Otway** of *Emma*. Her youthful liking for the name may have been destroyed when it was used by Samuel Egerton Brydges for the hero of *Arthur Fitz-Albini*, published in 1798, of which she had a poor opinion.

Augusta

The name Augustus had been conferred by the Senate upon the second Caesar and his successors, meaning revered or set apart, conferring majesty without royalty. It was not used again until taken up in the middle of the 16th century by minor German princes for their children, in both the masculine and feminine versions. The latter arrived in England with Augusta of Saxe-Gotha, who married Frederick Prince of Wales in 1738 and became the mother of George III. He named one of his six daughters after her, Princess Augusta born 1768. The name was a ridiculous pretension in the daughter of a lowly merchant such as **Augusta Elton**, *née* **Hawkins**, of *Emma*. It is doubtful whether **Augusta Sneyd**, acquaintance of Tom Bertram in *Mansfield Park*, has any better claim to it, in character if not in birth.

In several respects *The Watsons* seems to be a precursor to *Emma*, not least in the resemblance between Mrs Elton and Mrs Robert Watson, Emma Watson's ill-natured, showy sister-in-law. Mrs Watson (herself named Jane) has pretentiously named her spoilt child **Augusta**, the name which Jane Austen subsequently transferred to the adult character when she reworked her material. (Emma, Jane, Augusta, Elizabeth and Robert are all names in common between *The Watsons* and *Emma*.)

Basil

The name of a non-scriptural saint, it fell largely out of use after the Reformation. It was used once by Jane Austen for 'old **Sir Basil Morley**' an acquaintance of Sir Walter Elliot's in *Persuasion*.

Bella, Belle

Diminutives for the four-syllable Isabella; **Bella Knightley** is a small child in *Emma*, so called, presumably, because her full name is such a mouthful, while Isabella Thorpe's siblings sometimes abbreviate her name to Belle.

Betty
Mrs Jennings' maid in *Sense and Sensibility* and one of the maids in *The Watsons* share this name, which by the late eighteenth century was regarded as fit only for servants.

Betsey
A diminutive of Elizabeth, more homely than Lizzy or Eliza, less servant-class than Betty, this is the name by which the child **Betsey Price** is known in *Mansfield Park*. Though boy children are often called by diminutives, most girl children in Jane Austen have latinate names, indicating some degree of pretension and spoiling. Betsey is spoilt in her own way, but there are no pretensions in the Price family; one cannot imagine any of the girls being named for their aunt Bertram, Maria. Indeed, the only 'a-ending' name in the household belongs to a servant who gives herself airs, Rebecca. Betsey's godmother is in fact her aunt Norris, so Elizabeth is probably Mrs Norris's name: she is the only one of the Ward sisters, because the eldest, not named on the first page of *Mansfield Park*.

Bridget, Biddy
The cult of St Bridget was very popular in England as well as Ireland, the country with which the name is usually associated. The earliest occurrence of Bridget as a Christian name was the youngest daughter of Edward IV, born in 1480, whereas it did not come into common use in Ireland until the 17th century, at the same time as Mary. In *Mansfield Park*, in a flight of imagination Mary Crawford cites Bridget, together with Eleanor, as suitably old-fashioned names likely to have belonged to former wives or daughters of Sotherton Court. Though the names are grouped together here, elsewhere Bridget does not seem on the same level as Eleanor for Jane Austen. In the juvenilia, a character so called is condemned by her name to an unheroic destiny: "alas! she was very plain & her name was Bridget... Nothing therefore could be expected of her - she could not be supposed to possess either exalted Ideas, Delicate Feelings or refined Sensibilities".

The diminutive, Biddy, seems even more hopeless. An old friend of Mrs Jennings, of lowly origins, is **Biddy Henshaw**, the diminutive (by which Mrs Jennings knew her in her girlhood: "Biddy Henshaw as was") intensifying the already prosaic and outdated aura of the name. As early as 1705, in Richard Steele's play The Tender Husband, a character so named is objecting "Did you ever meet with an Heroine... that was termed Biddy?"

Caroline
In Italy the name Carlo (Charles) was feminised in two forms: Carolina and Carlotta, which became in English Caroline and Charlotte (qv). Both were imported into England via Germany by royal brides, the wives of George II and George III respectively. Jane Austen used the name for the snobbish **Caroline Bingley** of *Pride and Prejudice* as well as for the non-speaking **Caroline Otway** of *Emma*. One of Jane Austen's own nieces (born in 1805 after the original writing, though not the publication, of *Pride and Prejudice*) was named Caroline Mary Craven Austen. In her case the name came from her mother's pride in being descended from a Governor of Carolina, Lord Craven. The name of the two states, of course, had been given in honour not of a woman but of a King, Charles IV of France.

Catherine
This seems to have been one of the neutral names, capable of bearing a diversity of characters, in Jane Austen's repertoire. There are two Catherines in *Pride and Prejudice*, **Lady Catherine de Bourgh** and **Catherine Bennet**, the latter always known as Kitty (qv). Lady Catherine's unpleasantness is in contrast to **Catherine Vernon** of *Lady Susan*, who is one of the few pleasant characters in that tale. (She also has a child of that name.) An interesting occurrence of the name is **Catherine Morland** of *Northanger Abbey*. We know that Jane Austen first called both book and heroine 'Susan', and only changed it after another novel of that name was published. Of course she need not have made the change, since the novel itself was renamed (possibly by her brother Henry for posthumous publication, as not long before her death she was writing of the novel as 'Miss Catherine') to make it more Gothic.

Charles
Introduced with the Normans from Charlemagne, its original owner, it was not much used in England until the Stuart kings made it popular. James I and VI named his sons Henry and Charles in an unsuccessful attempt to avert the doom that had followed the six successive owners of his own name. By Jane Austen's day, it was one of the classic boys' names. She bestows it on a sprinkling of minor characters, predominantly pleasant but unremarkable men. It is the name of **Mr Bingley** in *Pride and*

Prejudice, though only his sisters call him so. Jane Bennet, who loves him, never refers to him as Charles even to her sister. The chief bearer of the name is **Charles Musgrove** of Persuasion, whose wife always calls him Charles. There are two, perhaps three more characters with the same name in this novel: little **Charles**, named after his father, and their cousin **Charles Haytor**. From his being so named we can deduce that Charles is also the name of old Mr Musgrove, and that the Haytors' eldest son is called after his uncle rather than his own father who is considerably lower down the social scale. To avoid repetition, Jane Austen could so easily have chosen a different name for this cousin that the duplication must have been deliberate. (Tom Haytor would be a fine choice in my view, while in the 1995 film he has been renamed Henry, obviously to avoid confusion, but thereby falling into an awkward and unnecessary Henry/Henrietta pairing.) Finally in the same novel is the deceased husband of Anne's old school friend, **Charles Smith**.

There is another **Charles Smith** in *Lady Susan*, an acquaintance of Reginald de Courcy, as well as the brother-in-law of the eponymous 'heroine', **Charles Vernon**. More non-speaking characters with this name are: **Charles Maddox** and **Charles Anderson**, both friends of Tom Bertram in *Mansfield Park*; from the same novel, **Charles Price**, a member of the Portsmouth family, **Sir Charles**, influential friend of Admiral Crawford and, at the other end of the social spectrum, the servant **Charles** who can be trusted to drive Mrs Norris to Sotherton. The non-commital nature of the name extends to **Charles Hodges**, who flirts with Isabella Thorpe in *Northanger Abbey*, and **Mrs Charles Dupois** of *Sanditon*. But everybody's favourite Charles must surely be the delightful ten-year-old **Charles Blake** with whom Emma offers to dance in *The Watsons*, thereby proving her good nature. Seen with a sympathy rarely accorded to the children in her novels, though almost always to the real-life children of her acquaintance, this young Charles may well be named for the only one of her brothers younger than herself, whose boyhood she observed from a different vantage point from any of the others.

Charlotte

Another Hanoverian introduction: Queen Charlotte was the German-born wife of George III. It is basically the same name as Caroline, both being feminine forms of Charles. Jane Austen seems to find the name pragmatic and unsentimental. These are the qualities in common between **Charlotte Collins**, *née* **Lucas**, in *Pride and Prejudice*, who marries knowing that her husband is a fool, and **Charlotte Heywood**, clear-eyed heroine of *Sanditon*. An exaggeration of this kind of character is **Charlotte Luttrell** of the juvenile fragment 'Lesley Castle', a young woman more interested in cooking than romance. But not quite all Jane Austen's Charlottes share this characteristic. **Charlotte Palmer** of *Sense and Sensibility* is simply silly, while **Charlotte Davis**, a Bath acquaintance of Captain Tilney in *Northanger Abbey*, is probably (for she is a non-speaking character) a common flirt.

Christopher

Belonging to the carpenter **Christopher Jackson** in *Mansfield Park*, the name was old-fashioned and rustic by this date, only fit for the lower orders. It was to fall yet further into disuse before it returned to favour. Fifty years after *Mansfield Park*, CMY writes, "Christopher was once far more common in England than it is at present". The name was not revived by the upper classes until the turn of the nineteenth/twentieth centuries, when it was borne by middle-class children like Christopher Robin Milne, who was so shocked, when he started prep school, to have to call the masters 'Sir', as this was how the gardener and chauffeur addressed his father!

Clara

18th century latinised form of Clare, used by Jane Austen for the mysterious **Clara Brereton** of *Sanditon* and for the undoubtedly shallow Bath friend of Mrs Elton, **Clara Jeffereys**.

Diana

A contraction of 'Diva Jana', goddess of the night, later more specifically of the moon, "her name slept," says CMY, "as a mere pagan device till the 16th century, when romances of chivalry gave place to the semi-classical pastoral". Diane de Poitiers, mistress of Henri II, made the name fashionable at the French court, whence it was taken up by the exiled English Cavaliers. However, for a long while it was confined mainly to a few aristocratic families, notably the Spencers and Churchills. When Jane Austen met somebody of that name, she found it worth remarking upon. In using it for **Diana Parker** of *Sanditon*, she was being curiously up-to-date, since it was in the same year, 1817, that Sir Walter Scott published *Rob Roy*, whose heroine Diana Vernon helped to spread the name among the general population.

Dick

An abbreviation of Richard, it is used by Jane Austen for children for whom she has little sympathy: **Dick Jackson**, the son of Christopher

Jackson, outdoor servant at Mansfield Park, "a great lubberly fellow"; **Dick Price** in the same novel; and the "troublesome", stupid **Dick Musgrove** of *Persuasion*.

Dorothy

The name not of a real character, but of an imaginary one: the "ancient housekeeper" conjured up by Henry Tilney to amuse Catherine Morland on their journey to Northanger Abbey. CMY says "Dorothy was once one of the more usual of English names; and 'Dolly' was so constantly heard in every household, that it finally became the generic term for the wooden children that [formerly] were called babies or puppets." 'Doll' also had a less pleasant connotation. "In the days of affectation, under the House of Hanover," CMY continues, "Dorothy fell into disuse, but was regarded as of the same old Puritan character as Abigail or Tabitha." That is to say that between its heyday in the 16th and 17th centuries and its revival in the late Victorian period it was regarded as old-fashioned or parochial; one of the few literate eighteenth-century holders of the name was Dorothy Wordsworth, born in Cumberland. Her niece and namesake adapted the name to the more fashionable-sounding Dora. In Jane Austen's time, the name may not have been pronounced as it has been since its revival. A children's grammar published in 1769 by Newbury, the same man who published the book 'Goody Two-Shoes' of which Jane Austen herself owned a copy, has the following question and answer passage:

Q. Does *h* never lose its sound after the *t?*

A. Yes, it is quite lost in these proper names, *Esther*, *Anthony*, *Thomas* and *Dorothy*.

Edmund

"There is nobleness in the name of Edmund," says Fanny Price. "It is a name of heroism and renown - of kings, princes and knights; and seems to breathe the spirit of chivalry and warm affections." This is the longest eulogy on any name by a character in Jane Austen. Of course, Fanny loves history almost as much as she loves her cousin. Two early kings of England and two saints had borne the name of Edmund. Not much used after the 15th century, it never became a commonplace name like the related Edward. It is, of course, the name of the 'bad' brother in Shalespeare's *King Lear*, yet of the good brother, **Edmund Bertram**, in *Mansfield Park*, a novel in which Shakespeare is mentioned. Because of the family relationships, this is a novel in which the hero is known by his Christian name throughout, so a slightly distinctive name is appropriate, but this may not have been Jane Austen's motivation in choosing it; we know that she had been partial to the name since her teenage years.

Edward

With Edmund, this was one of the very few Old English names to survive the Norman Conquest, the survival of both being the consequence of their being saints' names. Edward was also the name of post-Conquest kings, and was always much more common than Edmund, becoming one of these classic English names that appeared neutral to Jane Austen, the name of one of her own brothers. She uses it for one solid hero, **Edward Ferrars** of *Sense and Sensibility*, and for two other sensible men, **Edward Gardiner** of *Pride and Prejudice* and **Edward Wentworth** of *Persuasion*. However, the name did not always bear this character with her, since she also bestows it on the ridiculous anti-hero of *Sanditon*, **Sir Edward Denham**, and on **Edward Thorpe**, brother of Isabella in *Northanger Abbey*.

Eleanor and Elinor

Both elegant, sensible and feeling young women in Jane Austen: **Eleanor Tilney** of *Northanger Abbey* and **Elinor Dashwood** of *Sense and Sensibility*. The latter is one of three sisters all with slightly romantic (as opposed to pretentious) names: the choice of their romantic mother, undoubtedly. Maybe Mrs Tilney was romantic too; it would seem to accord with the circumstances of her life, and the name of one of her sons, Frederick, was romantic at that date. The Eleanor crosses, erected in memory of his wife by Edward I, lent romance to the name. CMY: "Eleanor continued to be a royal name as long as Plantagenets were on the throne, and thus was widely used among the nobility and afterwards by all ranks, when of course it lost its proper spelling and was turned into Ellinor and Elinor, still, however, owning its place in song and story." See also under *Bridget*.

Eliza

A fashionable abbreviation of Elizabeth in Jane Austen's youth; her worldly cousin, born Elizabeth Hancock 1761, was invariably known as Eliza. In *Sense and Sensibility* there are two **Eliza Williams**, mother and daughter, in Colonel Brandon's history. In *Pride and Prejudice* Elizabeth Bennet is called Eliza by female contemporaries but Lizzy by her family - the one form fashionable and the other familiar. (We cannot imagine her being called Betty.) But already by Jane Austen's maturity Eliza had fallen out of fashion, and the two Elizabeths of her last two completed novels are never called Eliza by their friends. A century later, and the name had descended right to the bottom of the heap - reference Eliza Doolittle, Cockney dustman's daughter of *Pygmalion*.

Elizabeth

The history of this name, one of the most popular in Jane Austen's day, is interesting. It did not become common in England until the end of the 15th century, when it largely ousted the medieval form, Isabel. The two names were interchangeable for a long period; in 1542 a Berkshire man named his wife in his will Isabel, while in her own will, dated two years later, she is named Elizabeth. There is only one English church dedicated to St Elizabeth and no surnames formed from the name (unlike Isabel, which has Ibson etc), two good indicators of medieval usage.

The new form was popularised by the great Queen Elizabeth, who had presumably been named after her grandmother Elizabeth of York. At the end of the 15th century it was still a comparatively rare name, but by 1560 accounted for 16 per cent of English female baptisms, and by 1600 by over 20 per cent, a position it held for the next two hundred years. By Jane Austen's day, therefore, it was one of the great standard names for girls, the name of two of her own sisters-in-law and of numerous acquaintance. Its popularity is acknowledged by her on the opening page of *Persuasion* when she details the Elliot genealogy "with all the Marys and Elizabeths they had married". The latest Lady Elliot had been an Elizabeth and so is her eldest daughter, **Elizabeth Elliot**, cold, haughty and self-centred. There could not be a greater contrast with the delightful heroine of *Pride and Prejudice*, **Elizabeth Bennet**. Jane Austen's well-known antipathy to Queen Elizabeth did not prevent her from using the name for one of her own favourite characters. In *The Watsons* **Elizabeth Watson** is kindly but not very refined, while **Elizabeth Martin** is the unremarkable friend of Harriet Smith in *Emma*. Four very different Elizabeths.

Emily

Chaucer anglicized the Italian Emilia into Emelye in his *Knight's Tale*. But it was never very popular in England until a daughter of George II, though christened Amelia, became known as Princess Emily. There was a second English princess of this name two generations later. Ann Radcliffe used the name for the heroine of *The Castle of Udolpho*, 1794, which is read so avidly by Catherine Morland in *Northanger Abbey*. The only **Emily** in Jane Austen's work appears in the same novel, being the non-speaking and non-surnamed new friend of Anne Thorpe.

Emma

The most prominent name in Jane Austen's *oeuvre*, in that it is the only Christian name appearing in a title. Attention is also called to the name by the pun made by Mr Weston during the picnic on Box Hill, when he asks which two letter of the alphabet express perfection (answer M, A). It is one of the few names for which we know Jane Austen's strong liking from her letters. Having abandoned the beginning of a novel in which the heroine was named **Emma Watson**, she kept the name for her next heroine but one, **Emma Woodhouse**. There are no minor characters by this name.

It is perhaps slightly suprising that Jane Austen was not put off by the notoriety given to the name in her lifetime by the mistress of Lord Nelson, Emma Hamilton. Though this was the name by which the world knew her, she had actually been born Amy Lyon, changing her name first to Emly, then, when she had learnt to spell, to Emily, and finally to the fashionable Emma.

Despite its similarity to the name Emily, Emma had in fact a completely different origin, having been brought into England by the daughter of Richard, Duke of Normandy, who married first Ethelred the Unready and second King Cnut. As a favourite Norman name, it gave rise to several surnames beginning 'Em' and a variant Christian name Emmet, before being abandoned as hopelessly old-fashioned. Unlike many early names that were revived under the Victorian taste for medievalism, Emma regained its popularity in the 18th century, no doubt because of its 'a' ending. Jane Austen encountered it in the character of Emma Bertram (evidently both names appealed!), heroine of Kotzbue's play The Birth-Day, which she saw in Bath in 1799.

The Victorians associated Emma not with its true Norman origin, but with its 18th century manifestation, so soon learnt to despise it whereupon it sank to serving-girl status.

Esther

An Old Testament name interchangeable with Hester. Like many Biblical names, it was not used in England until the 17th century; its heyday was the first half of the 18th century, and by Jane Austen's time it was beginning to feel dated. She uses it only in her unfinished fragment *Sanditon*, for the not very sympathetic character **Esther Denham**.

Fanny

This was one of the most popular names during Jane Austen's lifetime, belonging to a favourite niece, a sister-in-law and several acquaintance. It was also the name of the most famous female novelist of Jane Austen's youth, Fanny Burney (though she published anonymously, the secret of her authorship was soon out). Other famous bearers of the name were the actress Fanny Kemble and the wife of Horatio Nelson. All girls and women named Frances seem to have been known as Fanny, without exception, however well-born - very different from the equivalents Elizabeth / Betty, Catherine / Kitty, etc. Perhaps as a consequence, Fanny did not become a serving-girl name nearly as quickly as all the other y-ending diminutives, but retained its dignity and class. Jane Austen uses it first for an unpleasant character, **Fanny Dashwood** in *Sense and Sensibility* (and in the same novel for Colonel Brandon's cousin); then for a heroine dear to her heart, **Fanny Price** of *Mansfield Park*; for the 'superior' **Fanny Harville**, who has died before the start of *Persuasion*; and finally with complete neutrality for **Fanny Noyce**, friend of Diana and Susan Parker in *Sanditon*.

In choosing Fanny for the name of the heroine of *Mansfield Park*, Jane Austen may seem to be choosing a name that appropriately infantalises its owner, yet its history and contemporary usage indicates otherwise. It is notable that Mary and Henry Crawford move straight from the correct 'Miss Price' to wishing to call her Fanny - there is no more formal Frances in between (although the narrator gives Fanny's mother her proper name, **Frances Ward**, on the first page of *Mansfield Park*). She is only infantalised when her father calls her 'Fan' - one of only two instances in all the novels of a girl's name being reduced to its first syllable (the other is Lydia Bennet's friend Pen Harrington - but there is no Nan, Bet, Sal or Peg).

Interestingly, the present-day Burney Society, founded to promote the work of Fanny Burney, had to drop the Christian name altogether from its title to avoid a rift between its UK and US divisions: the UK preferring Fanny as more historically correct, the US insisting on Frances as more politically correct. In the 1995 film of *Persuasion*, Fanny Harville's name has been changed to Phoebe, for reasons we might guess, though evidently a similar change was considered too drastic for the 2000 film of Mansfield Park, in which the whole tenor of the principal character was changed, but not her name!

Fitzwilliam

The only use in Jane Austen's fiction of a family surname used as a Christian name, though several of her own acquaintance were christened on this principle. The mother of **Fitzwilliam Darcy**, hero of *Pride and Prejudice*, was Lady Anne Fitzwilliam. The Fitz prefix, a corruption of the French 'fils', indicates that somewhere along the line the family descended 'on the wrong side of the blanket' from royalty. During Jane Austen's lifetime a son of the reigning monarch, the Duke of Clarence, fathered ten children on the actress Dora Jordan, bestowing on them all the surname 'Fitzclarence'. One would not have expected Jane Austen to associate one of her most upright heroes with either Frenchness, royalty or bastardy, but as we have seen, this had been a favourite name since girlhood.

Flora
The name arrived in Scotland from France with the Stuarts and remained essentially Scottish, Flora Macdonald, the Jacobite heroine, being a prominent bearer of the name. Jane Austen uses it for Mary Crawford's friend Lady Stornaway, *née* **Flora Ross**, whose names proclaim a Scottish background. (see also *Janet*)

Frank
Jane Austen's brother Francis was invariably known as Frank. Similarly, **Frank Churchill** of *Emma* is never referred to as Francis. Like Fanny (qv) it would seem that Frank, as a diminutive, broke all the usual rules.

The name is also unique in Jane Austen's repertoire in suggesting a moral quality. She uses this to ironic effect in *Emma*. Frank Churchill, while having the demeanour of perfect frankness, is in fact master of deception and double-dealing.

Frederica
Feminine form of Frederick, used infrequently in the 18th and 19th centuries. **Frederica Vernon** in *Lady Susan* is presumably named after her father, since her mother, the widowed Lady Susan, ostentatiously makes a fuss of one nephew, Frederic, "for his dear uncle's sake".

Frederick
That this was one of Jane Austen's favourite names for men is suggested by the spoof entry she made in her father's register of a marriage between herself and 'Henry Frederic Howard Fitzwilliam'. **Frederick Wentworth**, loved by Anne Elliot in *Persuasion*, is perhaps the hero with the greatest desirability and sexual presence in all the novels. Jane Austen also uses the name for one of her most untrustworthy male flirts, **Frederick Tilney** in *Northanger Abbey* - like Wentworth, Tilney is a Captain, but in the Army rather than her esteemed Navy. I wonder whether Jane Austen knew at conscious or subconscious level of the real-life connection between the names Frederick and Tilney. Camden, in 1605, says 'For *Frideric* the English have commonly used *Frery* and *Fery* which hath been now a long time a christian name in

the ancient family of Tilney, and lucky to their house as they report'. A Fred. de Tilney is recorded as early as 1360. But the name, which is of course Germanic in origin, became generally popular in England only with the Hanoverians, Frederick Prince of Wales being son to George II and father to George III. As we have seen above, Jane Austen also used the spelling **Frederic Vernon** for a child in *Lady Susan*.

George

George Knightley, hero of *Emma*, the perfect English gentleman farmer, is perfectly named, since not only does the name derive from the Greek word for farmer (literally 'earth-worker', the first part of the name being the same as in Geography' and 'Geology') but it belongs to the patron saint of England. Despite seeming quintessentially English, the name was actually slow to be adopted in the British Isles. St George himself was a Roman, martyred in the East in 303. His cult was brought to England by the Crusaders, who felt he had come to their aid at Antioch in 1089, and there are 126 churches dedicated to him. Edward III had a particular devotion to him and founded the order of the Garter on St George's day (23 April) 1349. Yet he named none of his seven sons George, and the only member of the Royal family to bear the name before the advent of the Hanoverians was George, Duke of Clarence, born 1449. In English life generally it remained very rare. CMY says, "Scarcely a single George appears in our parish registers before 1700" and the lack of surnames deriving from it proves it was not in use in medieval times. It was only when George I ascended the throne in 1714 and began an unbroken succession of King Georges that the name became acclimatised in England. George III himself, because of his plain tastes and liking for the country, was often called 'Farmer George'.

Jane Austen's father, born 1731, was named George - a name completely new to the Austen family at that date. It came to him from his maternal grandfather, Sir George Hampson (who was certainly born before 1700) and passed on to his second son, who sadly grew up to be mentally defective and played no part in family life. Jane's brother Edward nevertheless named his own second son after his father, and the infant's pronunciation of his own name, "Itty Dordy", is recorded affectionately in one of Jane's letters. In *Northanger Abbey*, one of the heroine's nine siblings, only four of whom are named, is **George Morland**, and a **George Perry** is referred to as a possible (but absent) dancing partner for Catherine. Jane Austen also uses the name for **George Wickham**, charming anti-hero of *Pride and Prejudice*, though the christian name is hardly used. Famously, Emma Woodhouse expresses perplexity about using the name George when she becomes engaged to Mr Knightley. Only his brother John addresses him as George. There is a second **George Knightley** in *Emma*, the third son of John, as well as the non-speaking part **George Otway**.

Georgiana

This eighteenth-century female derivative of George (probably pronounced Jor-jane-a) belonged most famously to the Duchess of Devonshire, who was named after her mother and grandmother, the latter born Georgiana Carteret in 1716. The only character so named in Jane Austen is **Georgiana Darcy** of *Pride and Prejudice*. We can speculate that Mr Darcy senior was called George and that having given his only son his wife's surname, he perhaps wanted to perpetuate his own name in his only other child. To add weight to this theory is the fact that George Wickham is his godchild.

Hannah

One of the many Biblical names which had been current in the 17th century but was no longer used by gentry families. Hannah More, the respected literary figure of Jane Austen's lifetime, was born in 1745. The name only exists in the English-speaking world, the Biblical character elsewhere being translated as Anne. The only **Hannah** in Jane Austen is the servant at Randalls in *Emma*, daughter of the Woodhouses' own coachman James: no surname is given.

Harriet

Invented in France as the feminine form of Henri, the name Henriette was brought to England by Queen Henriette Marie, French wife of Charles I. As well as the anglicization to Henrietta, the sound of the name suggested Harriet to English ears, and both versions gained currency through the next two centuries. Alternative spellings were Harriot (a family connection of Jane Austen's was so named) and Harriette, while the diminutive became Hatty or Hattie. Jane Austen used the straightforward version for **Harriet Smith** in *Emma*, **Harriet Morland** in *Northanger Abbey*, and for two separate friends of Lydia Bennet: **Harriet Forster** and **Harriet Harrington**. The name seems to have suggested shallowness to her.

Harry

In Jane Austen's time a diminutive not of Harold, as it later became, but of Henry, and familiar from Shakespeare's history cycle: "Cry God for Harry, England and St George!" It was possible, but rare, for the name to be given in its own right, as it often is today. But perhaps **Sir Harry Denham** of *Sanditon* was never a Henry. Harry Musgrove in Persuasion is the youngest of a large family and, we are told, "much petted". Another spoilt child is **Harry Dashwood** of *Persuasion*, whose "imperfect articulation, earnest desire of having his own way, many cunning tricks and a great deal of noise" secure the favour of his great-uncle and the Norland inheritance. Not all Henrys were reduced to Harrys even in childhood. We do not hear of Jane's brother Henry being so called. Neither is the other child Henry of the novels, Henry Knightley. However, his uncle does have a manservant at Donwell called **Harry**.

Henrietta

It is **Henrietta Musgrove** and her sister Louisa in *Persuasion* who cause Admiral Croft to "wish young ladies did not have so many fine christian names". Both names, as feminine versions of male names with a French provenance, were relatively new and highly fashionable, perhaps alien to the Admiral's ear. They do not seem likely choices for the down-to-earth Musgrove parents to have made for their first two daughters, but they suit the characters of the girls, who are modernising their family, very well.

Henry

With eight King Henrys stretching from the 11th to the 16th centuries, this was one of the oldest-established English names, still very common in Jane Austen's day. It was the name of her own fourth brother, whose cleverness seems to find an echo in both her principal Henrys: **Henry Tilney** of *Northanger Abbey* and **Henry Crawford** of *Mansfield Park*. As both men have sisters, their first names appear frequently on the page, in contrast, say, to that of Mr Knightley, or even Mr Darcy. We know that Emma's father is **Henry Woodhouse** because he mentions that his eldest grandchild **Henry Knightley** was named in his honour. Two Henrys of rank are the deceased **Sir Henry Russell** of *Persuasion* and the **Sir Henry** who was one of the players at Ecclesford in *Mansfield Park*.

Hetty

In the eighteenth century Hetty could be a pet form equally of Henrietta and Hester. **Hetty Bates** is better known to us as Miss Bates of *Emma*. Her mother does once, rather touchingly, refer to her daughter as Hetty - reminding us that once the old lady is gone, there will be no-one to call Miss Bates by her Christian name. Jane Fairfax never says 'Aunt Hetty'. So was Miss Bates christened Henrietta or Hester? As the daughter of a clergyman, belonging to an unpretending family, and born perhaps about 1760, the

Biblical Hester seems more probable.

Isabella

When the fashion for choosing names for girls with the 'a' ending occurred in the eighteenth century, the longer form of the old name Isabel (which had largely died out in favour of Elizabeth) was found to be ideal, having the added advantage of 'bella' meaning beautiful. The name seems highly suitable for the smart, vain, flirtatious **Isabella Thorpe** of *Northanger Abbey*; less so, perhaps, for *Emma's* home-loving (though elegant) sister **Isabella Knightley**. Mr Woodhouse confesses that his elder daughter was nearly called Catherine after her grandmother. Perhaps Isabella was Mrs Woodhouse's name; more likely the Woodhouses decided to abandon family names altogether and choose names they simply found attractive for their much-loved daughters.

Jack

Workaday name derived from John. Its similarity to 'Jacques', the French form of James, has caused some confusion as to its derivation, but in *The Pedigree of Jack and of Various Allied Names*, 1892, E. Nicholson has shown its descent through Johannes, Jehan, Jan, Jankin, Jackin and Jack. The process was complete by the beginning of the 14th century, by which time Jack was already established as a synonym for man or boy. The OED gives no fewer than 80 uses and compounds of jack as a common noun. Though one of Jane Austen's earliest scraps is entitled 'Jack and Alice', in the mature fiction she uses it only once, for **Jack Stokes**, a working man mentioned in *The Watsons*.

James

Despite two saints of this name, numerous church dedications and several surnames, James was popular mainly in the north of England and in Scotland, until it was brought thence by the Stuart kings. Often spelt Jeames, it was so pronounced, according to CMY, "in the best society until the end of the last [i.e. eighteenth] century". It was brought into Jane Austen's family on her mother's side, the Leighs, her eldest brother being named in honour of his wealthy uncle James Leigh Perrot. In the novels there is no major character with this name. The most prominent is **James Morland**, the heroine's eldest brother in *Northanger Abbey*. Though he might seem to have little in common with the clever James Austen, in fact both men were curates, sons of clergyman, eldest of large families, and liable to fall in love rather too easily in their youth. Otherwise, Jane Austen seems to use the name indifferently just when a Christian name is required for some character usually known by his surname: **James Brandon** in *Sense and Sensibility*; **James Rushworth** in *Mansfield Park*; **James Benwick** in *Persuasion*, for example. **Sir James Martin** is a fop in *Lady Susan*, and **James Tomlinson** a neighbour in *The Watsons*. Then there are three servant **James**: the coachman of both Mr Woodhouse and Mr Watson, and the manservant of Reginald de Courcy in *Lady Susan*.

Jane

Joan was the popular form until the sixteenth century when, under the influence of Jane Seymour and Lady Jane Grey, it began to be superceded by Jane, which by the 18th century was almost as popular as Elizabeth, Mary and Anne. Jane Austen had many relations on both sides of her family, including her maternal grandmother, named Jane. She could hardly escape being so named. After her birth, her father writes that she is going to be known as Jenny (which in that era may have been pronounced Jinny); there is no further evidence of this, however, and it seems certain that the pet name did not survive her infancy.

She seems to have used her own name for fictional characters without identifying them with herself in any way. Of the two sisters at the heart of *Pride and Prejudice*, it is Elizabeth, not **Jane Bennet**, who shares some of her author's characteristics. The inscrutable **Jane Fairfax**, though admirable in some ways, is nothing like her author, and we are never privileged with her point of view. How can Jane Austen bear to have her own Christian name bandied about so in the mouth of Mrs Elton? Speaking of whom, there is her prototype the vulgar **Jane Watson** of *The Watsons*, and the non-speaking **Jane Fisher**, a visitor to Sanditon, to make up Jane's tally of Janes.

Janet

The Scots form of Jane, Jane Austen uses it with a cluster of other Scottish names for **Janet Fraser**, *née* Ross, one of two sisters who are Mary Crawford's pre-Mansfield friends.

Jemima

An Old Testament name, one of the three daughters of Job, its a-ending formation perhaps delayed its slipping down the social scale, though eventually it was to do so. In 1801 Fanny Burney chose the name for a perfectly well-bred young lady in her play *A Busy Day*. In 1816, Jane Austen's niece Anna Lefroy gave birth to a daughter whom she named Jemima, a name that was in her husband's family, the Lefroys. (Like most Huguenots they favoured Old Testament names and were using Isaac and

Benjamin after other gentry families had dropped them.) At around the same time, however, of rural stock in Dorset, was born the Jemima Hand who was to become the mother of Thomas Hardy. Jane Austen uses the name only once, for **Jemima** the young Musgroves' nursemaid in *Persuasion*. This Jemima is a servant, but one who gives herself airs.

John

Undoubtedly the preponderant male name in England (and in its various forms elsewhere in the Christian world) through many centuries. Its peak of popularity came in the second half of the 17th century, when more than a quarter of all boys in England were baptised with this name. The fact that there were two major saints named John - the Baptist and the Evangelist - and that both had two feast days, could not but have helped to increase the incidence of namesakes. Even in the period 1750-99, when most of Jane Austen's acquaintance and characters would have been born, John accounted for nineteen percent of male baptisms.

It does not seem to be a name she favoured. Her only 'good' John is **John Knightley** of *Emma*, and even he is not wholly likeable. There is also a young **John Knightley**, the second son of John Knightley senior, and in the same novel is **John Abdy**, ostler of the Crown Inn struggling to maintain his elderly father in addition to his own family, and **John Saunders**, presumably a blacksmith. There are two servants named **John** in *Pride and Prejudice*, belonging to the Collins and the Gardiners. Hovering on the edge of gentility, **John Shepherd** is the agent for Sir Walter in *Persuasion* and **John Price** is one of the Portsmouth family in *Mansfield Park*. Two gentlemen of the name make prominent appearances in *Sense and Sensibility*: **John Dashwood** and **Sir John Middleton** (and his son of the same name). Then there are three rather villainous Johns: the horrible **John Thorpe** of *Northanger Abbey*, the **Hon. John Yates** who brings theatricals to Mansfield Park, and the worst scoundrel of them all, *Sense and Sensibility's* **John Willoughby** - though his Christian name might be anything, it is so little in evidence.

Julia

A literary name, appearing in Shakespeare and Herrick, but not adopted as a name in real life until the 18th century vogue for a-ending names caught it up. It still had a literary flavour, however, and Henry Tilney speaks of the name being common for heroines of sentimental or Gothic novels. In *Mansfield Park* I always think this ought to be the name for Mary Crawford, whose attractiveness could use a more sparkling and unusual name. It is somewhat wasted on **Julia Bertram** herself. Having named their elder daughter after her mother, I wonder where the Bertrams found the inspiration for Julia? (If Miss Crawford had been Julia, the second Miss Bertram could with great plausibility be Elizabeth, after her aunt Norris.)

Kitty

Kitty Bennet of *Pride and Prejudice* is invariably known by the diminutive of her real name Catherine, just as Elizabeth is known as Lizzy within the family. But these forms were rapidly becoming dated and before long would be associated only with old women. It is notable that in her juvenile fragment 'Catharine, or The Bower', written in 1792, Jane Austen refers to her heroine as Kitty throughout, except in the title and opening sentence, whereas Catherine Morland of *Northanger Abbey*, prepared for the press in 1816, is never so named, even by her family. The rhyme 'Kitty a fair but frozen maid' reminds Mr Woodhouse, in *Emma*, of the fact that his eldest daughter 'was near being called Catherine after her grandmama'. CMY says that Kitty, for Catherine, "was almost universal in the last century". Kitty Fisher, of nursery-rhyme fame, the mistress of several eminent men, died in 1767.

Letitia

The Latin form of the older name Lettice, neither ever very common. Jane Austen uses it in the fragment *Sanditon* for the minor character **Letitia Beaufort**.

Lewis

The English spelling of the French Louis, it was associated with the Normans, as is the surname of the only character to bear the name in Jane Austen's novels, **Sir Lewis de Bourgh** of *Pride and Prejudice*.

Lizzy

See Elizabeth

Louisa

A name not known before the 18th century, derived through the French Louis and Louise. Louisa Countess of Berkely, born in 1694, the granddaughter of Charles II and his mistress Louise de Keroual, was one of the earliest bearers of the name. From its aristocratic beginnings, by the end of the century it had reached the ordinary members of the gentry who sought fashionable names for their daughters (and, according to Henry Tilney, novelists for their heroines). **Louisa Hurst** of *Pride and Prejudice* would have been born about 1770, **Louisa Musgrove** of *Persuasion* a generation later in 1795. Admiral

Croft was still finding the name strange and difficult to remember in 1814!

Lucy

From the 12th century, Lucy was a favourite name in England. "Most popular in the 17th century, when many noble ladies were called Lucy," says CMY. As the 18th century ran its course, however, the name suffered the usual fate of y-ending girls' names and slipped down the social scale. In *Sense and Sensibility* it is just right for **Lucy Steele**, therefore: slightly vulgar, but not so much so as her elder sister Nancy, being at least a name in its own right and not a diminutive. The other bearer of the name is also struggling at the lowest reaches of gentility: **Lucy Gregory**, a Portsmouth girl mentioned by William Price in *Mansfield Park*.

Lydia

The name came into use in England in the 17th century, and was made famous by Sheridan's Lydia Languish (The Rivals, 1775), some of whose giddy qualities and eagerness for elopement are shared by **Lydia Bennet** of *Pride and Prejudice*. Lydia is the only one of the five Bennet sisters not to have a standard English name; had her parents followed their usual pattern she must have been Anne, but this might not have been characterful enough for her creator. As the only Lydia of the novels, she certainly stands out, and together with her literary namesake, has made the name difficult to choose for subsequent generations.

Margaret

One of the oldest English names, associated both with saints and royalty, and giving rise to more than 30 surnames, proof of its ancient lineage. A daughter of Henry III was christened Margaret because her mother had invoked the saint during labour. Queen Margaret was the wife of Henry VI and her name was made familiar to later generations by Shakespeare's play. Margaret Beaufort was the mother of Henry VII and her grand-daughter, Margaret Tudor, was the last royal Margaret until the twentieth century. Among the general population it rather fell out of use in the 18th century and we can imagine that when the Dashwoods chose it for their third daughter - **Margaret Dashwood** of *Sense and Sensibility* - the name would have had for them a romantically old-fashioned appeal. It retained its favour in Scotland and **Margaret Fraser**, step-daughter of one of Mary Crawford's friends in *Mansfield Park*, is given a name that enforces the Scottishness of the whole family. The name is also used in *The Watsons* for one of the sisters of a not at all fashionable, hardly genteel family, **Margaret Watson**.

Maria

Pronounced Mar-eye-a from the time of its adoption in the 18th century; only in modern times, under the influence of foreign travel, has the middle syllable sounded 'ee'. **Maria Bertram** of *Mansfield Park* takes her name from her mother, **Maria Ward**, so named in the first paragraph of the novel. Other bearers of the name are **Maria Lucas** of *Pride and Prejudice*, **Maria Thorpe** of *Northanger Abbey*, and **Maria Manwaring** of *Lady Susan*. Shallowness is the quality that unites all these young women and it seems to have been a name for which Jane Austen could feel no respect. She may rather have despised it as a modern - and to some extent foreign - perversion of the honest, time-honoured name Mary. Certainly CMY has something sharp to say on this score: "Our Latin Maria is a late introduction, brought in by that taste which in the last century made everything end with 'a'; when, as Scott laments in *St Ronan's Well*, Mary lost its simplicity and became Maria; but this affectation is happily falling to the ground".

Marianne

Marion or Marian, which had since the Middle Ages been a pet-form of Mary, acquired two more letters in the 18th century and transformed itself from a medieval nickname into a fashionable amalgam of Maria and Anne. **Marianne Dashwood** of *Sense and Sensibility* is unique in Jane Austen's work in bearing this name.

Martha

A name that never escaped its housewifely connotations from the Biblical character, though often paired with Mary in families of sisters. Jane Austen knew sisters named Martha and Mary (both married brothers of hers as their second wives) but though she was particularly fond of her friend Martha Lloyd, she presumably felt her name was not worthy of her, since she used it only for the non-speaking but undoubtedly vulgar **Martha Sharpe**, friend of Anne Steele in *Sense and Sensibility*.

Mary

First found as a Christian name in England at the end of the 12th century, Mary became hugely popular, giving rise to many surnames and having twice as many churches dedicated to this saint than to the next most popular, Peter. Not surprisingly, the name suffered an eclipse after the Reformation but it gradually came back into use until by the middle of the 18th century nearly 20 per cent of English women bore the name. Two of Jane Austen's sisters-in-law were called Mary, as were numerous acquaintance. Twelve of her own characters are Mary, not 20 per cent of her total, but far more than any other single name. Most prominent is **Mary Crawford** of *Mansfield Park*, whose name seems too commonplace for such an exotic import into Northamptonshire. Next is **Mary Musgrove** of *Persuasion*, followed by **Mary Bennet** of *Pride and Prejudice*. **Mary, Lady Middleton** of *Sense and Sensibility*, **Mary Edwardes** of *The Watsons* and the two **Mary Parkers**, mother and daughter, of *Sanditon* are all minor characters. The remaining Marys are non-speaking parts: **Mary King** who flees Wickham in *Pride and Prejudice*, **Mary Price**, Fanny's dead sister in *Mansfield Park*, and three from *Persuasion*: **Lady Mary Grierson** and **Lady Mary Maclean** both referred to in other people's conversation, and the **Mary** who is servant at Westgate Buildings. The profligacy with which Jane Austen bestows the name on her characters reflects the name's prominence in reality, as does their owners' social range from Earl's daughter to servant.

Matilda

There is no real character called Matilda in the novels of Jane Austen, but as part of her spoof on the fashionable Gothic novels, she uses it for an imaginary character in *Northanger Abbey*. It had been very popular in the 12th and 13th centuries, giving rise to surnames such as Tilson and Tilney. Having fallen out of use for several centuries, it was revived in the 18th under the dual influence of fascination with the Gothic and taste for the a-ending. It was the name of a play performed by the Austens when Jane was a child. She used it frequently in the Juvenilia, but presumably thought it too extreme for her later fiction.

Nancy, Nanny

The early diminutives of Anne were Nanny or Nan, but these came in time to be terms for a loose woman, and were replaced in the 18th century by Nancy. By the end of the century however this too was rather questionable, and when in *Sense and Sensibility* Lucy Steele calls her sister Nancy she is either unconsciously betraying her own vulgarity of thought or consciously seeking subtly to demean her sister. Either error is avoided by the narrator who always calls **Nancy Steele** by her real name Anne, or by the socially correct term Miss Steele. Nanny meanwhile was acceptable only for a servant; there was such a one at Steventon, and both the Watsons and Mrs Norris of *Mansfield Park* have a maid called **Nanny**. This did not, of course, imply the care of children, as it would now; that usage came in later.

Patty

A diminutive, together with Matty, for Martha (cf. Meg and Peg for Margaret, Molly and Polly for Mary). Jane Austen's own friend Martha Lloyd was never (as far as we know) referred to by either diminutive, which by the late 18th century were confined to servants. In *Emma*, **Patty** is the Bates's hard-worked (though kindly treated) maid of all work, a particularly suitable name since the Biblical Martha was notable for her diligence with the housework.

Penelope

The name of the faithful wife of Odysseus was first used as a Christian name in England in the 16th century, having formerly been popular in Ireland and brought thence by Penelope Devereux, friend of Philip Sidney. Jane Austen uses it for two rather ill-bred characters: **Penelope Clay** in *Persuasion* and **Penelope Watson** in *The Watsons*. The original Penelope's perseverence finds an echo, albeit a twisted one, in the perseverence that both these characters demonstrate in their quest for a man to keep them. A friend of Lydia Bennet is **Pen Harrington**, the contraction adding to her vulgarity and inelegance.

Philip

This name of an apostle was common in England in the Middle Ages, hence the number of related surnames. But its popularity waned after Philip of Spain, the husband of Mary Tudor, became seen as England's enemy. Why Jane Austen should choose this name for **Philip Elton** in *Emma*, whose Christian name is mentioned only once, is obscure; perhaps it was a name she particularly disliked.

Rebecca

As with many Old Testament names, Rebecca's peak of popularity was the 17th century, and by Jane Austen's day it was decidedly old-fashioned. Her own paternal grandmother was Rebecca. Charles Lamb associates it with Quakers in his 1809 poem, and CMY says "It is spelt both ways [Rebecca and Rebekah] by those who bear the name, who are chiefly of the lower orders and generally called Becky". Thackeray was to use this diminutive, of course, for his 1812 heroine on-the-make in *Vanity Fair*. Though Rebecca had slipped to the servant-girl class in Jane Austen's time, its a-ending suggested a servant who gives herself airs: just right for **Rebecca** the Prices' servant in *Mansfield Park*.

Reginald
A Norman name which conveyed its hint of chivalry to the character **Reginald de Courcy** in *Lady Susan*; in fact two characters, father and son.

Richard
In the first paragraph of *Northanger Abbey*, we hear that the heroine's father 'was a very respectable man, though his name was Richard'. This seems to have been a family in-joke. Despite its being such a common male name, Jane Austen has no major character called Richard, only an array of non-speaking parts: the above-mentioned **Richard Morland**, **Richard Thorpe**, also of *Northanger Abbey*, **Richard Price** of *Mansfield Park*, **Richard Hughes** of *Emma*, **Richard Pratt** of *Sanditon*, and in *Sense and Sensibility* a cousin of the Steeles named **Richard**. (Though he is given no surname he too might be Richard Pratt, since the Steeles have an uncle of that name.)

Robert
Another very common male name all through the centuries from the Conquest onwards. Neither **Robert Ferrars**, of *Sense and Sensibility*, nor **Robert Watson**, of *The Watsons*, is an attractive character, while *Emma's* **Robert Martin** might be a solid and worthy young up-and-coming farmer, but his voice is never heard in the novel. In *Mansfield Park* the Grants' gardener is called **Robert**, making this another of the names that would fit either servants or gentry. At the other end of the social scale is **Sir Robert** of *Sense and Sensibility*, uncle to the Ferrars.

Sam
After the Reformation Samuel became a favourite choice for boys, but by Jane Austen's day it had a working class ring about it. Samuel Johnson (born 1709) came from lowly stock (his brother also had a Biblical name, Nathaniel) and Samuel Taylor Coleridge (born 1770) positively detested his first name. Jane Austen uses it for rather low-born characters: the young sailor **Sam Price** of *Mansfield Park*; **Sam Watson**, brother to the four Watson sisters, who is "only a surgeon", not good enough for Mary Edwardes; **Sam Fletcher**, friend of John Thorpe; and 'old **Sam**', servant at the hotel in *Sanditon*.

Sarah and Sally
By the late 18th century both the Old Testament name and its common diminutive had a distinctly old-fashioned feel. In the second chapter of *Northanger Abbey* **Sally Morland**, Catherine's next sister, changes her name to **Sarah** in a perhaps vain attempt to be more fashionable or more dignified ('for what young lady of common gentility will reach the age of sixteen

without altering her name as far as she can?' asks the narrator). In this instance she must be reverting to the name by which she was christened and growing out of the pet-form used by her family - as perhaps Jane Austen herself grew out of Jenny, and Elizabeth Bennet out of Lizzy. All the rest of the Sallys and Sarahs in the novels are servants. **Sarah** is the name of the elderly nursery-maid at Uppercross House in *Persuasion* and of one of the Longbourn maids in *Pride and Prejudice*. **Sally** is the name of the second Portsmouth servant in *Mansfield Park*, a servant of the Middletons in *Sense and Sensibility*, and a maid of Mrs Forster in *Pride and Prejudice* again. Jane Austen herself knew several maids with the name of Sally, as well as one daughter of a vicar (the Revd Peter Debary) who did not object to being called Sally though her real name was Sarah. Sarah Siddons, born 1755, was a generation older than Jane Austen, by whom she would have been regarded as barely genteel.

Selina

This name appears to have been a 17th century invention, its dual roots being an anglisiation of the French Celine and an adaptation of the Greek word for the moon. Selina Finch, born 1680, married the 1st Earl Ferrars and her daughter Selina Shirley (1707-1791) became the Methodist Countess of Huntingdon, whose chapel in Bath, just across the road from the Leigh Perrot home in the Paragon, Jane Austen would have known well. In giving the name to **Selina Suckling** in *Emma* she seems to be choosing names for the two Hawkins sisters as pretentious as she can make them.

Sidney

This was an early example of a surname becoming a Christian name in general use, not confined to certain families. Her choice of the name for the possible hero of her last (uncompleted) novel, *Sanditon*, **Sidney Parker**, may owe something to the famous wit Sidney Smith, her own contemporary. Sydney Place, Bath, Jane Austen's address from 1801 to 1804, was named in honour of Thomas Townshend, 1st Viscount Sydney (1733-1800) as was the convict settlement in New South Wales to which her Aunt Leigh Perrot was very nearly deported!

Sophia

Meaning wisdom, its use as a Christian name derived from the dedication of the Christian temple in Constantinople. A Hungarian princess was so called in 999. Its use gradually spread across the continent and it was introduced to England by the Royal family, notably through their German connections. An early example was the youngest daughter of James I, born in 1607, named after Anne of Denmark's mother Sophia. Though she lived for only one day, there is a sculpture of her in her cradle in Westminster Abbey. Writing of the estranged wife of George I, CMY says "though the unhappy Sophia Dorothea of Zelle never took her place in the English Court, her grand-daughters made it one of the most fashionable ladies' names under the House of Hanover; and though its reign has passed with the taste for ornamental nomenclature, yet the soft and easy sound of Sophy still makes her hold her own". Henry Fielding chose it for the heroine of *Tom Jones*, 1752. 'Sophia Sentiment' is the *nom de plume* of the writer of a letter to James Austen's Oxford-based periodical *The Loiterer*; the teenaged Jane Austen has been suspected of being its true author.

Sophia Croft in *Persuasion* is rather strangely named; one would have expected a less fashionable and sentimental name. Her husband's remark on the difficulty of remembering names like Henrietta and Louisa: "I should never be out, if they were all Sophys or something of that sort," would have more meaning had his wife been plain Mary or Jane. But it is nice to hear him call her by the affectionate abbreviation of her name. The other two Sophias of the novels are both rather low: **Sophia Grey**, the inferior but rich wife of Willoughby in *Sense and Sensibility*, and Anne Thorpe's new Bath friend, probably as vulgar as she is, **Sophia** in *Northanger Abbey*.

Stephen

The name of the first Christian martyr, it was very common in the Middle Ages, as the number of surnames deriving from it attests. Falling into disrepute after the Reformation, by Jane Austen's day it was rarely used by the gentry, and is used by her for two servants. Admiral Crawford's man in *Persuasion* and one of the grooms or postilions in *Mansfield Park*.

Susan

A contraction of the Biblical Susannah, Susan became a name in its own right from the 17th century, becoming very popular in the 18th. It would seem an unpretentious name suitable for an unaffected sort of girl such as **Susan Price** in *Mansfield Park*, and it was also Jane Austen's first choice for the naïve heroine of *Northanger Abbey*. However, **Lady Susan Vernon** in the novel that bears her name could not be a more different type of character, scheming and manipulative. There is something of this too in **Susan Parker** of *Sanditon*, though without the deviousness.

Thomas, Tom

One of the half dozen most common men's names in England over several centuries from the 13th to her own time, Thomas was used by Jane Austen both for gentry and servants - but notably, never for a hero. It is the name both of the Dashwoods' manservant in *Sense and Sensibility*, and in *Emma* of the servant of either Frank Churchill or his father. It is notable that they are called Thomas, not Tom as one might expect. **Thomas Palmer** is a minor character in *Sense and Sensibility*. The only major characters to bear the name are **Sir Thomas Bertram** and his son **Tom Bertram**; it is almost as if Jane Austen was reserving the names for them. There is no other name and its diminutive (assuming she wished son to be called after father, yet to be distinguished from him) that would give at once the dignity of Sir Thomas and the immaturity of Tom - the latter helped by Fielding's *Tom Jones*. Tom seems the archetypal name of fallible but often disarming male youth: though Tom Brown, Tom Sawyer and Tom Tulliver were all to come later, of course.

The Bertram influence spreads to Portsmouth where there is a young **Tom Price** in the family; in the same novel there is a young man **Tom Oliver**, friend of Tom Bertram. **Tom Musgrave** is the immature and swaggering anti-hero of *The Watsons*; the name is just right for him too. In the last fragment, *Sanditon*, the enthusiastic promoter of the resort is **Thomas Parker**.

Walter

Introduced at the time of the Conquest, the name was infrequently but steadily used through the centuries. It was often pronounced with a silent 'l' as was Ralph, another Conquest name. Towards the end of Jane Austen's life the fame of Sir Walter Scott began to increase its popularity until it became a typical Victorian name. **Sir Walter Elliot** and his little grandson, **Walter Musgrove**, are Jane Austen's two bearers of the name.

William

From the 16th to the 19th centuries William averaged 20 per cent of male baptismal entries in English parish registers, tying with John for first place. Jane Austen uses it for the extreme of attractive and unattractive characters. **William Price** of *Mansfield Park* is the former, **William Collins** of *Pride and Prejudice* the latter. *Persuasion's* **William Elliot** (who has dropped his middle name Walter) has his agreeable qualities but is ultimately found to be "black at heart". **Sir William Lucas** of *Pride and Prejudice* is harmless but vacuous, **William Coxe** in *Emma* is "a pert young lawyer" while **William Thorpe** of

Northanger Abbey is probably no better than the rest of his family. There is a child by this name, **William Middleton** of *Sense and Sensibility*; a servant, General Tilney's man **William**; and a member of the working classes, **William Heeley**, shoemaker of *Sanditon*.

> *My name is Diana; how does Fanny like it?*
>
> **Letters**

> *"I wish young ladies had not such a number of fine Christian names. I should never be out, if they were all Sophys, or something of that sort."*
>
> **Persuasion**